The Key to Life is...

BALANCE

Definitely Balance is what it is all about. The great thing about Melissa Stone's new book is it is practical, easy to use and it works! It is a must read for anyone and everyone.

--Lee Holden
Director: Santa Cruz Chi Center
Author: Seven Minutes of Magic

As a family doctor, I am very excited to have this workbook as another tool for patients and myself. Melissa's personal style draws you in, and her weekly topics are simple yet mighty. It is a great introduction to basic spiritual principles and the exercises are quick enough that even the busiest person can find time to do them. The beauty of her creation is that anyone who will put in even a few moments of willingness to participate will have enormous return from the insight they gain. Melissa has written this workbook to help people bring balance into their lives, which it certainly does. What is so interesting to me is that the organization of the book itself is a demonstration of balance; truly a reflection of the author and her intention.

--Amy Solomon, MD
Local Family Practitioner

Books have always played an important role in my life. As a youth one of my favorite activities was going to the library and searching through the shelves for numerous books that would open doors that would reveal new and wonderfully exciting information. I have always considered the best of these books like friends who you would enjoy visiting. I have now added Melissa's wonderful new book to my stack of special friends. To know Melissa as I do as a kind, caring, considerate and compassionate individual who feels like your most comfortable chair in how she offers you exactly what you need while asking little in return prepared me for what I was about to experience. Her book is like a wonderfully detailed travel guide that makes your journey through life so much easier to take by giving you the tools you need to live peacefully, joyfully and with optimal health. This is the type of book that I love to offer to very special friends as a gift that will have a positive influence in many aspects of their lives. I am honored to have Melissa Stone as both a friend and inspiration as I grow and strive to become a wiser and more understanding practitioner in the healing arts. Her book deserves a special place in my library.

--Richard Goldberg
Nutritionist, herbalist, teacher, writer, researcher, movie producer

Melissa Stone's book lovingly reminds us that our state of being is up to us, and provides practical steps to get us more into that balanced moment of being.

--Michelle DeAngelis
President of Michelle Inc. and Founder of Planet Joyride; Author of Get The Life That Doesn't Suck

The organic miracle of life is balance. It is THE lesson we all have to remember. Melissa's book helps you become aware of life's greatest miracle. On any level this book can help you. Want to start with your thinking, your feelings, or your actions? Wherever you are, Melissa can help you begin to live your life in balance. Have fun with it!

--Larry Bernstein, CST CPT Fsoc OB
Director and Instructor of Cypress
Health Institute

In her clear, down-to-earth, and loving voice, Melissa Stone offers a welcome new guide to personal well-being and abundance. Melissa speaks from a place of great integrity and compassion-both for herself and for others. She also speaks from a place of great courage – it is through her willingness to share and fearlessly explore her own process of self-transformation that we receive this gift of her new book. Herein she offers creative, inspiring, supportive – and yes, balancing, meditations, exercises, and processes – all designed to point us gently, yet firmly towards our own authentic selves.
Gasshô, Melissa !

--Tracey Kahan, Ph.D.
Associate Professor of Psychology
Santa Clara University

Everyone needs a little positive affirmation sometimes but why not challenge oneself with a year's plan for positive change. Reading and applying the daily OMs in Melissa's book, "The Key to Life is... Balance" is a daily reminder on positive outlooks to replace those neglected aspects of life and to finding a path that leads to the natural self.

--Liliana
Editor-In-Chief, Belly Dance Magazine

There are the senses you get and then there are the senses that get you. Being around Melissa, I get the sense that I am connected to someone who is in process of transcendence. Do you remember when you were a kid and your buddy dared you to touch the tip of your tongue to the 9 volt battery? It is kind of like that, but all over your body. Tingly, Powerful! The energy is incredible and now I understand how Melissa has become that way. Melissa shares intimacies about her journey out of suffering and how her awareness is allowing her to not only experience all she can while she is here, but to pass on the Landmarks of her Journey to others and help them to end their suffering as well. A truly epic in the tale in Spiritual Growth and a sense which got me. ".

--Trevor Bottorff, RRW, CSC
Chemical Dependency Residential Case Manager Certified Spiritual Counselor

10/08

Christina,
Enjoy!
Love you!
Peace,
Melissa

Dragonfly Publishing Company
Felton, CA

"The Key to Life is...Balance"

Requests for information should be addressed to:
Dragonfly Publishing Company
www.dragonflypublishingcompany.com

ISBN # 1438242034
EAN-13 9781438242033

printed in the United States of America

~   ~   ~   ~   ~   ~   ~   ~   ~   ~

Cover design by Gary Winnick, www.Lightsourcestudios.com

Interior Design & Editing by Debi Burdman-Deutsch

The Key to life is....

Balance

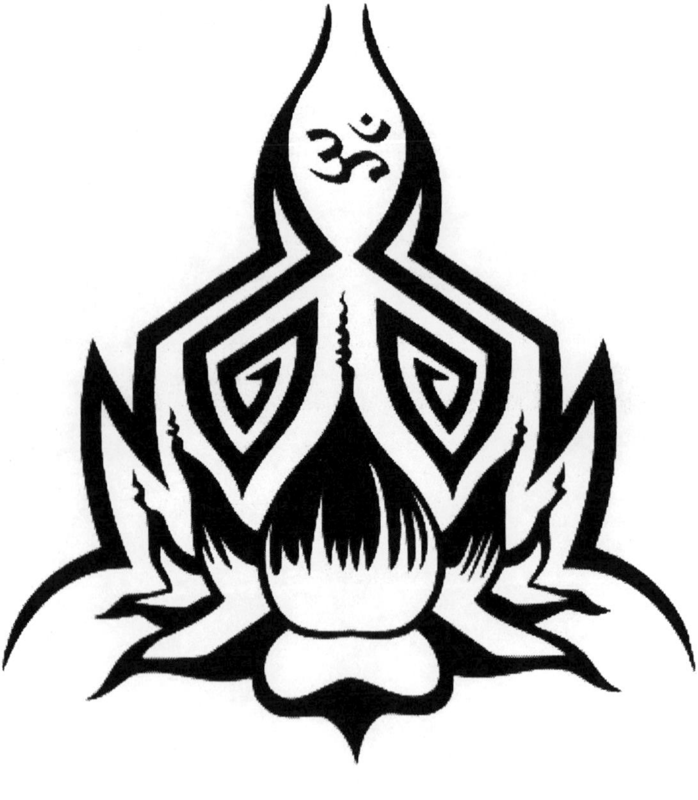
ॐ

Balance is:

a: physical equilibrium
b: the ability to retain one's balance

Life is like riding a bicycle. To keep your balance you must keep moving.
--Albert Einstein

Our lives are a mixture of different roles. We are complex and have many talents and the ability to wear many hats.
--Melissa Stone

The Key to life is....

Balance

Weekly Oms to help you find Balance...

One year of inspirational, spiritual passages with a workbook to help you close the gap, start walking your talk, feeling completely totally alive and in balance.

Get Balanced! Find Peace of Mind, Body and Spirit!

By: Melissa A. Stone
CMT and Fitness Professional

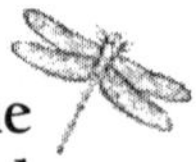

Contents

Contents [continued]

~ ॐ ~

Namaste'

I Honor the place in you in which the entire Universe dwells.
I Honor the place in you which is Love, Light and Peace.
When you are in that place in you and I am in that place in me
We Are One!

A

Acknowledgments

I thank and appreciate all spiritual beings, living and passed on. To those that have touched my life: without you, I would not have written this book or be the person I am today. All the teachers, healers, lovers, friends, family and God - we truly are one, Namaste'.

To those I have yet to meet and that will touch my life in the future: I honor you and wait to see what pleasures and lessons you bring to me. It is through the experience of others that we grow and learn to love/live life to its fullest.

Dedication

For my Mom, as she taught me the hardest lesson of them all and I love her for it!

For Hailey N. Stone, the most beautiful spirit I see!

For my dog Max, who is always sitting beside me.

For all my cats past and present for the comfort and purring you gave me in my time of need.

For Sally's family: her mother and her father, her brothers, her grandparents, every aunt, every uncle and all the cousins; you gave me a sense of what a family is, and you gave me love when I needed it most, during the holidays. I appreciate you all and send you joy and love.

Introduction

My intention in every word written here is to help anyone that is ready to heal past wounds and move to present moment. For anyone that wants to live, feel and be in balance with harmonic wealth. When we are open to healing and can find how to live in the present moment, there is no struggle and life flows like the river. The key is balance with and in everything you do. We create our own reality; we must take responsibility for where we are in life and for our karma. We need to do the work and feel the pain to be able to move it out and release it.

This book is how I did the work from my rock bottom to where I am today. I had many books, classes and experiences, some of which I have listed in the back of this book. I feel that I have come up with simple and easy ways to process your past emotions, look at your life, your path and to help you in healing it all. It has taken four years to organize all of these simple and easy ways into book form. I believe that with this book your life will change with each week as you look at how you are addressing each emotion, situation and how your energy flows. This is what we are all looking for: an easy way out or that magic pill. I will say this many times in the book: there is no pill that will help us lose weight, love ourselves or find our purpose. It is all about having the courage to keep going and start over every day, if need be, to live only in the present and to learn to enjoy each moment of the journey. This book can give you the weekly courage to do this and more.

How to use this book: begin on a Sunday; read the Om, then each day do the exercise that goes with the Om. It will take less than thirty minutes a day I promise or do more and achieve change faster.

I hope that from my experiences you too can find your way to peace and living with love, that you will be able to speak your truth and find your authentic self. To get up every day and love what you do and do only what you love.

While in massage school, another student told me that she admired me for living each moment to the fullest. That was the first time that I had heard anyone say what I was striving to achieve and since then I have heard it a lot. This will happen to you again and again if you focus on changing your habits. Others will notice and so will you.

1

Four years have passed since I thought of writing an article called "Weekly Om". It is spring. I am broken hearted. Another relationship has ended, but somehow I know it was to end so that I could finish this book and clear out some old emotional patterns. What I do best is turn my negativity, my pain into something positive. I love to write and this book has been sitting half written for over two years. With tears streaming down my face and love in my heart for someone that can't love me back, I pick you back up, my "Weekly Oms." Creating something wonderful from the pain I am feeling, hoping it will help others and in turn help me.

In the last ten years I have come to realize that it is my calling to help others feel hope, love and comfort. It is my gift and my path.

When I ponder all that I have looked at and worked on, I feel and see that I have come a long way. I am not even the person I was back then. I now speak my truth and walk my talk. I see only the potential in everyone including myself. No dream is too hard to achieve and the universe is on my side.

I do feel the fear in others and in myself, sometimes so deeply that it knocks me off balance. When it does, my spirit takes over and lifts me back up. Fear is what knocks us all off balance. It is just so hard to see it when you are disconnected and in the midst of stress or chaos.

I have been working with people with addiction for the last four years. I have learned a tremendous amount from working with addiction. It is just creative energy that is misused. Most of these people are empaths but don't know it or what that means. When creative energy is not used to create in the positive it will create in the negative instead, as self-destruction.

I am an empath as well, which means that I am a person who is able to sense the emotions of others or who feels a lot! I feel everything...sometimes it becomes so overwhelming. At times I have a hard time in large groups of people. Having no manual on being an empath, some turn to drugs and alcohol to numb the feelings and pain they feel - not realizing that that pain might not even be theirs. Sometimes making up in their heads why they feel this way; creating stories, mis-communications and other negativity. Ever had a loved one or friend tell you that you did something that you never did? This is a story created from feelings they feel. It could be an old feeling coming up or someone else's feelings they were feeling. It's all energy and it's running through each of us. If you are open you will feel it all. That is why we all need to meditate, to process what we are feeling before jumping to conclusions.

In order for me to stay in balance I need to quickly process a lot of stuff, as I am around a lot of people in healing mode. I need to keep moving, meditating and loving myself to stay present. Sounds like a lot of work, right? It really isn't. If you do the work in this book and get yourself to a place of knowing what you are like when in a negative state, you can design the path to get yourself back in balance quickly. Develop a support group of people that can give you positive feedback when you are being your "old" self. Get some body work, eat a great healthy meal or take a long hot bath. Read and do the work and check out the exercises for more quick and easy ideas on how to get yourself back in balance.

Through all the hard work I have realized that I chose to live a childhood with no love or affection, and to have the many failed love relationships with the men unavailable to me. I had these experiences so that I can help others, and to write this book. This is my purpose and I have been told this in many strange ways; from strangers and through my own dreams. I am done learning the lessons; I have it figured out so this is why this book can finally be finished.

Taking risks is scary but this is the only way of really succeeding in life. If I had listened to those who told me not to quit my day job over four years ago I would not have done all that I have done and would not be where I am now. Staying stuck in the safe place has never appealed to me; life never changes and you cannot grow. The growing keeps us young and vital and feeling like we are living life to its fullest. When we stop growing we stop living and then when we get old and life is about pain and suffering instead of peace and euphoric joy. Our souls want us to live life to its fullest, to experience all that we can in the time we are here.

I have always felt I am here to leave a big imprint, one that succeeds more than just this generation. I have held in my heart from a very young age that I would somehow write a book about my life experiences that would help many. I remember, as young as five, being fascinated with anything having to do with the metaphysical world. I was called a day-dreamer by teachers but in reality I was staying connected with the spiritual world and teaching myself meditation. I feel that I am an old soul; one that has been here many times and lived many lives.

I was born without any privileges of material wealth and was raised by a single mother who could not show love. I went through many hardships always feeling very alone and unloved. With all of my self-discovery, I have learned that I am not alone and that I am loved and I have many gifts to offer. As we all are loved and have many gifts to offer.

I had a normal family life: Sunday dinners at grandma's and family holidays, and I felt loved - until the age of six. One gloomy spring morning I asked my

3

mother if my Nana was going to die. She seemed shocked at my knowing such a thing, as it was all being kept secret from my older brother and me. Being clairsentient and sensitive I am able to just know things. My Nana died some months later and I was not told for two or three days, but I knew. When my grandmother died I went inside myself and did not let anyone in. She appeared to me in her bedroom weeks after her death. I wish that I could remember more details of that day. I only remember that I felt, smelled and saw her and it scared me. My family life fell apart after this but the lessons of my life began. My Nana was my world and the only one in my family that could show me love and talk to me about spirituality. I remember always looking at this picture of Jesus in The Bible as she told me the story of his life, and she always sat with me to recite my nightly prayer. All of this stopped when she died, and for me: I feel my Spirit died with her. I have spent the last ten years reconnecting with it as I healed my pain and my life.

This last relationship woke me up. I did not want to continue on this path of heartbreak. I wanted.... 'Harmonic Wealth'. I had already succeeded in the four elements: spirituality, health, mental and financial. Just one part held me back from having the harmonic wealth that I wanted to experience - the relational one. It is our birthright to have all five of these elements, that is balance at its fullest and when you have all five you are at peace and feel joy. Living life to its fullest and feeling totally alive.

By feeling alive I do not mean you will never feel pain and or have a bad day. Feeling totally alive means you will be present in all of it and not have to hide or deny any part of your life. You can show the world your authentic self. You see pain as something you must go through to learn a lesson, to grow and to become stronger. The best part of doing the work is you will also see and feel more love and joy in your life. This love will flow from you and you will stop looking for outside things to comfort and love you. You will understand what present moment feels and looks like. You will also be able to handle things like sickness, death and heartbreak when others need you.

The death of my grandmother and loss of family love created this person in heartbreak. I was programmed to believe that I am not worthy of love and of being loved. I looked for and attracted those that kept me in this heartbroken space, my place of comfort. I stand now on the first step, thinking that I can now start asking the question. The answers will lead me to a way to stop the patterns and I will make better choices towards love, the love of myself.

Why do I attract things that keep me in heartbreak?

4

It's late on a Saturday afternoon, I am still writing and pondering this question and it comes to me in a flash. I take everyone at their word; I think they all walk their talk as I strive to do. I never ask anyone, "Do you walk your talk?" I just assume others are striving at living in balance and in the present moment like me. If I make it clear and ask in the beginning would the outcome be different? Realizing this was a big 'Ah-HA!' moment for me. Walking your talk means that everything you say, you actually do and want. There is no gap between what you say and what your actions are. When you can walk your talk you leave only positive energy, you have fewer disagreements with others and people can trust you. Along with walking your talk you must have open communication with everyone, speaking only truth. This is difficult but needs to be done in order to keep your energy and the energy around you clear and calm. Speaking the truth is hard for people to do because they are afraid to hurt others, so they tell half truths or say what the other wants to hear to keep peace. Telling someone the truth can be both hard to say and hard for them to hear, but it keeps trust alive and energy clear.

This journey of my self-discovery began in 2000 after a verbally abusive relationship ended. This was rock bottom for me. I allowed myself to move in with an alcoholic. My intuition told me not to do it, but my ego told me differently. After only several months I looked into the mirror not recognizing the person looking back. I did not like myself and wondered, "How did I get here?" Instead of blaming the other person I was looking at how I got myself there. I was grateful to have heard this within myself, because it got me out of it fairly quickly but not without a huge negative imprint in my life and my daughter. This is what changed me and what started all my healing.

One night sitting under the redwoods, after a huge fight where my boyfriend trashed our home I cried and asked, "God, help me come back to my spirit... to be the person I will love again." This journey went through many twists and turns but was so worth it. I feel now that I have cleared out my pain, my karma and I am now the authentic person that I can love. Along this journey I realized my path is to teach what I have learned and that is when I changed my career after twenty years.

One winter's day in 2004, I decided to write a column. I called it "Weekly Om" and I sent them out each Sunday to my clients. The word **Om** (aum) derives from the Sanskrit language. The Om is the primordial sound by which the earth was created- a similar concept to the Greek Logos. It symbolizes unfolding or expansion - when pronounced, it begins in the lungs, and ends on the lips. It is a symbol that is used in Yoga to describe the four parts representing the four states of human awareness:

The Om (Aum)

Part one:

The ordinary waking or material state:

Part two:

The state of deep sleep, or meditation:

Part three:

The dream state or a manifesting place:

Part four:

The absolute conscience or the awakened state.

These Oms represent all my self-discovery, my lessons and all my pondering questions and insights over my years of healing. I wrote this column for over one year, creating fifty two inspirational spiritual passages. Not really knowing what to do with them, they would sit for almost three years, while I learned more lessons and discovered how to put them all into a book. All of the Oms, meditations and articles that I have written are my own expression of the lessons that I have learned and the truth that I know. I believe they all come from Spirit, The Universe or God (whatever you call it) as they are all one and the same - as we are all one and the same.

With all of this I have learned if you want something for yourself, you will need to share it with others. This is my gift to the world, with hopes that it will help you in living in balance and feeling totally alive. I believe when we all get in balance there will be peace in our world. This will be my goal: "World Peace!"

~ I love this quote:

Be the change you would like to see in the world
--Gandhi

I would love to see in this world a place where we are not afraid to love and live. To love ourselves and everyone around us, to live with compassion for those we do not even know.

Neale Donald Walsch is an amazing man and he writes in his books "Conversations with God" that there is only fear and love. This is so true!

When we choose fear we cannot grow and when we choose love...well it's a beautiful thing. Right now the world is mostly in fear-driven by media and government in full-fledged greed. When we are in this place we are listening to our ego and not our spirit. The energy that is created is negative and creates pain and suffering.

Just realizing your pattern gives you hope of a new start and the releasing of something that no longer serves you. The first step to opening up to the spirit letting it lift you up towards a place of lightness, letting you feel like breathing again and being in a loving place no matter what is going on around you. Do you feel this at times? If only we all could stay in this space we would live in a life filled with love, success and abundance. It can and is happening to others, should we not all have this?

I hope after reading this book you too can be on the path of balance in your life.

When you are in alignment and working towards achieving this balance what you think about will manifest into reality. I remember sitting with my boyfriend at the time, when I started to write the Oms. We were talking about dreams and plans and he said "One day you will have a radio show." I laughed, and said "I am not looking for one." – but thought to myself it would be fun. Well guess what happened?

About two years later one fell into my lap.

This past year I had the honor of co-hosting, a one hour radio show on a local talk radio AM station with my friend, Sophy Winnick. We created a show based on sending out goodness into the world and enjoying the sweetness in life. We called the show "Radiance and Chocolate" the name given to us by the station but so fitting for what we wanted to create.

The enjoying part really happened for me when the show ended as the station was full of negativity being mostly a news talk station. We were breaking new ground of being positive in a negative space, so every Monday we would put on our white light and go in to battle the negative forces and talk about things the station and most listeners did not understand. The honor and pleasure came from the guests we had on the show and the whole experience of learning how to produce the show and of course the running of the board. I certainly learned a lot.

Our past guest list included local guests - Richard Goldberg - Herbalist, Dr. Amy Solomon MD, Jan Rekoutis - Astrologer, The local Wildlife Rescue, Bigfoot Museum, both Rev. Andrew and Kelly Springer. We did speak to some not so local guests and our own mentors and heroes - Dr. Bob Sears MD, Jenn Kober - comedian, Greg Fitzsimmions - comedian, Kristin McGee – MTV's Yoga instructor, Joanie Greggains – Fitness Professional and Radio Talk Show Host, Jack Lalanne – The Guru of fitness, Shakti - Singer, Neale Donald Walsch – Author of Conversations with God, Jeff Tyman – The Peace Troubadour, Dannion Brinkley – Author of Saved By The Light, Anodea Judith – Author and teacher of Chakras, Charles Muir teacher of Tantra and we had booked when the show was cancelled James Von Praagh - Medium and co-producer of "The Ghost Whisperer" and Debra Katz – Author of "You

Are Psychic". Our fun times with musical guests - DJ Namaste', Keith Taylor, Braddah Timmy and The Cocktail Monkeys.

One of the guests really put it in simple terms for me. Her name is Michelle DeAngelis creator of Planet Joyride – www.planetjoyride.com. Michelle said on the show: it's all about walking your talk and closing that gap between not doing it and doing it and the AHA moments being when we wake up a bit and come closer to closing that gap.   Thanks Michelle and keep up the joy ride!

I hope this book gives you many AHA moments and helps you to close that gap.
I guarantee that if you read the Oms, do the workbook and meditations at the end of one year, you will find yourself stronger, more clear-minded and focused. Feeling healthier, happier and more at Peace. You might even be able to manifest your own reality.

Feel free to read all the Weekly Oms in one sitting, one week at a time or do both.

I promise that if you make the commitment to spend one year learning, growing and being present you will find yourself more at peace.

*I am in balance with the
universe and its will
--Anonymous*

Chakra System Chart

Chakra is a Sanskrit word, meaning spinning wheel or vortex. It is a system that contains our energy force running up the midline of our bodies. This book contains information about The Chakra System, what the Chakras are, and how they help to balance out energy. This system is amazing and complicated; I tried to slowly dive into it throughout the book, keeping it simple. If at any time you do not understand please go to this page, diagram and reference. Be patient; after finishing the book you will have a general knowledge of this great energy system.

Sahasrara
Ajna
Visuddha
Anahata
Manipura
Svadhisthana
Muladhara

The Seven Chakras

Muladhara~ Root Chakra (base of tail bone) grounding and our support system

Svadhisthana ~ Sacral Chakra (below the navel) your emotions and pleasure

Manipura ~ Solar Plexus (below the breast bone) personal power and your will

Anahata ~ Heart Chakra (center of chest) unconditional love

Visuddha ~ Throat Chakra (base of throat) speaking your truth and freeing creativity

Ajna ~ Third Eye Chakra (center of forehead) intuition and inner vision

Sahasrara ~ Crown Chakra (top of head) spirit or higher power and knowledge

~ ॐ ~

Positive Thoughts - What Are You Creating?

Positive thoughts are thoughts that will bring you closer to happiness and peace. It takes work, self-esteem and unconditional love to always keep the healthy thoughts. Our surroundings, people and our situations sometimes pull us from our path creating negative energy that will turn our thoughts from the positive side.

Do you ever notice that when you think about what you don't want to happen, it does? When creating negative experiences in your mind you are giving the universe permission to manifest all of the fears and thoughts into reality, as energy knows no right or wrong. The Law of Attraction says that "What you ask for you will get." When it happens we think, "See that's what I was afraid of." Yep, it sure was.....you just received what you asked for.

What if you took all the time and energy and thoughts as the best positive experience instead of the negative one or the one of fear? Wouldn't you then manifest the best positive experience? Think about this.

The first step to creating a positive thought pattern is by creating a trigger that tells you that this is only a negative thought and not reality. Responding with a positive thought instead, you will have to work hard at it for a while, but then one day it will come to you on its own. You will be thinking about yourself in a negative way or being in fear and boom... your internal talk will say "No", giving you the automatic response and positive reinforcement you need to move out of the negative space. This takes focus and strength to get to this space and we all have the power within ourselves to accomplish this.

You will start to remind yourself of the beauty that lies inside and see that there is a silver lining in every cloud. You will start to see sadness, ugliness and pain all around but you can be at peace with it, knowing that it is as it should be in this moment. Accepting that we all have to go though the hard and tough times in order to really appreciate the good and knowing what we are not. You will start letting go of worrying about what we cannot control and knowing that we all have our path to follow and our own lessons to learn.

One Love, One Heart,
One World
--Unknown

13

We are all beautiful in our own way, each of us holds the piece of the kaleidoscope that when placed together becomes us, the world.

Start on your path to Peace by beginning to change your thoughts to be more supportive and positive. Notice the signs of the universe as it brings in people, situations, material things and even animals into your life. For only one reason and that is to manifest your thoughts into reality. If this is the truth and it is, then why are we causing the universe to help us to manifest bad situations, worry and fear?

Change your path and make it your mission to create thoughts of a more positive nature, once your karma is cleared the universe and energy currents will follow, thereby shifting the situations to positive ones. Creating Abundance!

Notes:

_____

_____

_____

_____

Positive thoughts - Workbook One

~Monday
Make at least one positive statement about yourself and post it to your bathroom mirror.
Say it out loud every morning before you get ready.

_____

_____

~Tuesday
Think of ten positive words to describe you.

_____ _____ _____ _____

_____ _____ _____ _____

_____ _____

~Wednesday
What is your least favorite thing to do at work?

_____

Make a list of things you can do to change that? (Listen to music while doing it, re-arrange your desk, bring in plants, and smile while doing the task.... etc)

_____ _____ _____

_____ _____ _____

~Thursday
Drive to work and notice five things that you like or are happy seeing during your drive.

_____ _____ _____

_____ _____

-Friday

Think of someone you have a strained relationship with, even if it is you. Write down five positive things that knowing that person has brought you, or things that you have done for the world.

_____   _____   _____

_____   _____

~ॐ~

Getting Yourself Back on Track – Are People like Trains?

My family has always had a love for trains. Growing up, my mom and uncle had train sets that they loved to get out every holiday season. My mom would tell me stories about my great grandfather the conductor from Pennsylvania and how she loved to ride with him. I, personally, loved the TV show 'The Wild Wild West', mostly because of the ending when they would get on the train.

Train rides are thought of as exciting and romantic adventures, invoking the feeling of freedom from within.

Look at your life from the perspective of the train and its tracks, you as the train and life as the tracks, the engineer is your brain and thoughts.

The train tracks stretch across the countryside, crisscrossing along - just as life reaches out - expanding energy to others. Trains make scheduled and unscheduled stops along the way. Life is always a balance between scheduled and the unscheduled. Some trains travel for hours toward one destination. Some casually wander from one stop to the next. The express train moves in a fast in pace from one stop to the other.

Where is the engineer of your thoughts taking you?

Is this the route or destination that you really want?

Only you are in control of the route, destinations and what stops you get on or off at. You can pick the places you want to visit and the ones where you want to call home.

Are you moving too quickly, like the express train? Or, Are you moving as a commuter train, traveling on the same routes over and over again?

Sometimes life happens even on a train.... I had an experience on a train ride coming home from vacation; my train hit a car. In seconds the lives of two were gone and the lives of hundreds were touched. Everyone on that train was re-examining the tracks of their life's moments after they heard of the fatality. We should all take time every day to keep the tracks on route, as a day by day process. Keeping this process will help in times of derailment. You will find the path more fulfilling if you stay on the tracks of prosperity.

Sometimes making that change in route, taking a different train, opening up to new experiences and places, will give you better insight to the real destination you are searching for.

Meditation can help you to see what route you are on.

Take time daily to slow down and check in with yourself.

Train Meditation – Do you see your tracks?

Lying or Sitting in a comfortable position being aware of breathing from your belly, as you inhale the belly rises and when you exhale the belly falls. Make sure you have a straight line of energy from the sacrum up through the crown, letting the shoulders fall away from the ears, lifting up through the breastbone and pulling the navel into the spine. See yourself as a train; see your life's tracks in front of you. Are you in a tunnel? Can you see your path or are you one of the other trains I described above? Follow the path as far as it takes. Focusing on your breathing until you want to come back then writing down what you experienced even if it makes no sense right now, it just might be that it is just around the bend.

Notes:

_____

_____

_____

_____

Getting yourself back on track – Workbook two

-Monday
What is your destination? Why?

____

____

-Tuesday
Thinking about your destination, is the track you are on the way to get there? If not, what is? If so, why?

____

____

-Wednesday
What stops do you need to take to help get you there? Make a list...

_______________ _______________ _______________

-Thursday
When do you think you might get to your destination? List the timeframes including your stops.

_______________ _______________ _______________

_______________ _______________ _______________

_______________ _______________ _______________

-<u>Friday</u>
Plan a trip that includes a train ride. As you step on the train take a deep breath and open up your mind -give yourself the freedom to enjoy the experience.

Do the meditation while on your train ride or for thirty minutes tonight.

~ ॐ ~

Affirmation – Creating Positive Change?

In the year 2000, I was able to buy a home; it was a rundown mess as my daughter put it. She was five when we found our selves homeless and in need of a place to call ours. I was blessed with a good job, good credit and an angel of a realtor. We were not homeless in the sense of having to live on the street thanks to all who gave us a place to sleep during that thirty-day period. It definitely was my rock bottom, *and* when my healing was to begin.

As soon as I got the key I started creating affirmations all over our new home.

--I stenciled on my wall of my living room "Live, Laugh, Love, Dance, Dream"–

and we built into the fireplace rocks that say words like "Love", "Dream" and "Peace".

This is how I started to create change by using affirmations.

An affirmation is a positive statement that helps to assert and influence thinking. Using positive statements as you self talk throughout the day, you are creating and cultivating this into a habit. Transforming the energy in the body with new interpretation of positively and/or healing.

I have found that through the daily ritual of affirmations or single positive words, I can create huge changes in my life. Making any change in life is hard and right when you want to give up, is when you need more than ever to keep it up. Finding a statement that you like can be a key to your success.

It can be fun to try and make up your own. Next time you meditate try to think of some positive things to say to yourself.

The Three Rules for Affirmations

A. No – no's or cant's - or No Negative words
B. KISS - Keep it Short and Simple
C. Everything Now - or in the present tense

Try placing the statements or words in places where you will see and read them - refrigerator, the mirror, in your car or in your garden. You can even put words into the décor of your home. It's fun and easy and the transformation will begin, guiding you to a more positive peaceful place.

Notes:

_____

_____

_____

_____

Affirmation – Workbook three

~Monday
Write five positive words to describe you.

_____   _____   _____

_____   _____

Write the first word on a post it note and place it where you will see it first thing in the morning, use this word all day when speaking with others.

How did you use this word today?

_____

_____

-Tuesday
Make a sentence with the second word describing you and put it as your screen saver on the marquee.

_____

_____

How did seeing this change your day?

_____

-Wednesday
Look up affirmations on your computer and find one that uses your third word or close to it. Print out that affirmation and post it on your fridge.

_____

How many did you find with your word in it?

_____

-Thursday
Think of someone else you know that has the same quality as your fourth word. Tell them you feel that way.

Who was it and why?

_____

-<u>Friday</u>
Make up your own affirmation using the fifth word. Post it in your car to see while you drive or somewhere in your house.

_____

List other affirmations that you made up and the creative ways you displayed them.

_____

_____

_____

~ॐ~

Weekly Om – Four

Present Moment – Are You Missing It?

I write this as I approach my 40th birthday and hope that this can be my present to all of you as you have all been a gift to me! I love what I am doing in my life and I am blessed to be able to be in the present moment to tell you about it.

*There is a Rainbow in the Sky
all the time.*
--Ziggy Marley

Life is full of wonderful things and horrible things all at the same time. Let's not forget we are at war, but the birds still sing and most of all our children still smile. Life is busy, stressful and full of electronic devices, all of which change the energy running through the body, taking us away from our true selves.

When you meditate you bring yourself back to what is important and that is getting in touch with *you* - bringing yourself back to the breath, so that you can appreciate the moment. When we are not in the present moment we are disconnected with our higher power, not at peace. Most important of all, we are not sharing peace and happiness with others. We get stuck in story-telling or finding fault when really none of that matters. Those we love or those we share living space with will pick up on our disconnect, and if they are not focusing they will then also disconnect.

When we are peaceful and happy we smile, we appreciate things, and we start to get creative. Feeling this way around our loved ones they will benefit from it as well.

In this day and age we are busy thinking about what we have to do and what we don't want to do. Many devices like TVs, cell phones and satellite dishes are taking away our energy without us even knowing it. Most of us do not know how to rejuvenate ourselves; we sit down in front of the TV or the PC thinking that this is relaxing. In fact it's taking more of your energy by emitting negative energy, noise and even violence into your body.

To get back to your true self you need to slow down, get grounded and breathe. This needs to happen at least once each day to keep the connection with your spirit and higher power. Even if it is just for five minutes each day, it will make a difference. You will see a bigger difference when you begin to take thirty minutes or more.

Just imagine a world where we all are at peace and happy living and enjoying the present moment; a world where we have learned how to work through our issues in a healthy manner and we stop getting stuck in bad situations. Where we can have open conversations and agree to disagree, instead of having a war. Peace it is not about going out and demonstrating against war.... that will not bring on World Peace.

It's within each of us and is our capacity of smiling, breathing and being at Peace with ourselves... that we can make Peace happen.

Peace starts with you and the finding of present moment and your higher power.

Grounding Meditation

Standing strong through the legs, lifting up through the breast bone and letting the shoulders drop down the back, try to wrap them around the shoulder blades, becoming strong in your core by contracting through the navel. Feel the whole foot on each side attaching to the earth, when you have that feeling see, in your mind's eye, roots coming from each foot and sending the root into the ground. Feeling strong, focused and connected to the Earth, in the present moment.

Notes:

_____

_____

_____

_____

Present Moment – Workbook four

<u>~Monday</u>
Write down 5 words that describe what the present moment feels like. If you
are not sure take a guess.

_____   _____   _____

_____   _____

<u>~Tuesday</u>
Remember the last time you really felt you
were connected and living in the present
moment.

_Every new day is a gift that's
why we call it 'the present'_
--Unknown

<u>~Wednesday</u>
Write about how you feel right now; and then do the grounding meditation
(see previous page) and write how you feel after. See any differences?

_____

_____

_____

-<u>Thursday</u>
Smile at ten people that you do not know today (in line at the store or gas station). How did it affect them? Do you feel you made a difference in their energy? Why?

_____

_____

-<u>Friday</u>
Do the grounding meditation all day when needed, and notice all things that are the color of red today, wear red or buy yourself some red roses.

~ ॐ ~

Healing – What is it, Really?

Healing is not just about the physical body or about the healing of symptoms. It can be a sense of healing the mind, body and spirit in its entirety, making whole.

We all have our issues to battle, negative feelings from time to time. I like to call these our lessons and I believe that when we learn the lesson, we gain the insight to moving beyond the negativity or the issue. We then can move past it unblocking it. Closing that gap and bringing us closer to our authentic self, our spirit.

Do you ever wonder, Why does this always happen to me? Do you find yourself in the same type of situations over and over again? Maybe you are missing the lesson... The other aspect is the physical pain and dis-ease that most of us carry around in our bodies. The dis-ease is the symptom brought on by the issue or negative emotion. When you are only healing the symptom you are not healing the issue that lies beneath the pain or blockage. This leaves you open to that pain or stress becoming chronic or causing additional dis-ease. We all laugh at the size of the booklet that prescribed medication comes with and the negative side effects given in the TV ads. That does not sound like healing to me! Might there be a holistic way to solve the underlying issue first?

An example of this is: I had a client that had a neck pain. She was suffering and came often for body work. She would tell me about the bad relationship she was in. One day I said maybe he is the pain in your neck. We laughed, she left him and her pain did go away.

The revelation of finding the root problem will enable the true purpose to be released and will allow deep healing to take place. The essence of the person, not the physical vehicle determines our standards even the most imperfect body with the spirit, shinning through, becomes beautiful!

Healing is Balance and Balance is Healing!
--Melissa Stone

Healing is at its best when the Root Chakra (at the tail bone) and Crown Chakra (top of the head) are in balance and in alignment. The following exercise is one to help with this.

Meditation to Connect the Root and Crown Chakras

Lying in relaxation with spine aligned palms up. Inhale into the Root Chakra. Send the breath up the spine through all the Chakras to the Crown. See the breath as white light as it flows up the spine. Then repeat in the downward motion. Continue the pattern until you feel and see it flow through the Chakras with ease.

Healing Pain Meditation

Focus on the place of illness or pain; draw a line around it making it a shape. As you inhale fill it with green energy and as you exhale see and feel the pain leave. Add in self-massage while doing the healing meditation or just resting your hands at the site of the pain will also help in the healing process.

*_Always seek medical attention if the pain persists or is too much for you to control in meditation_

Notes:

_____

_____

_____

_____

-<u>Monday</u>
Make a list of things or relationships that are not working in your life right now.

_____   _____   _____

_____   _____   _____

See if you can list reasons why.

_____   _____   _____

_____   _____   _____

-<u>Tuesday</u>
Take the first 'item' off your Monday list and think; then write up a plan to shift that to a more positive situation, leaving out any excuses why you can't achieve it. You should feel like all resources are at your fingertips. What would you do to change that item?

_____

_____

_____

_____

-Wednesday
Book a massage with a therapist or trade with a friend or your spouse. Most malls now have a chair massage place -- book fifteen minutes, if you have time or currency issues.

-Thursday
Do the Connection of Root and Crown Chakra meditation within this Om. When you feel a clear flow of breath and rhythm, ask for what is needed to make the shift of energy for first item on your list. Do this for all items on your list. See if you can restore balance within this flow.

-Friday
Make notes of any shifts in energy. Is there still pain in the body where it was before?

If so, do the connection meditation from Thursday and the following healing meditation for thirty minutes.

_____

_____

_____

~ ॐ ~

Obstacles – What Are Your Excuses?

When I finally was able to look at my excuses I could see how they all held me back and kept me stuck. I was always the victim and it was always someone else's fault that I was in any given situation.

My huge and first real self achievement was that of losing weight and changing my body. All self was motivated by just wanting to be thin. Later I would learn that being thin was really not what I wanted at all. Being healthy was much more important. Of course this realization would take years and would be the start of it all.

When it comes to making positive changes in our lives, like starting a new fitness practice or changing your diet, we tend to sabotage by making excuses. We all know that if we are taking care of ourselves... we look and feel better. Did you know that our bodies are made to move and food is our fuel? If you are not moving every day stretching out each body part and moving each joint, you will become stiff and the joints will start to hurt. Just like the Tin Man in the 'Wizard of OZ'. Feeding your body food that will not support it, by not supplying it with nutrients, it will start to fail.

Would you put sugar in your gas tank?

Are the excuses just us being stuck in the comfortable place of not loving or giving to ourselves? We then make up excuses and they feel like truth.

A successful fitness practice can give you stress reduction, heightened awareness, and greater flexibility and can be personally meaningful. Your body will love you if you start to move it. In order to get this wisdom and understanding you need to get rid of the excuses of why you can't have it.

What are your excuses?   _____

_____

Yoga Journal listed these as obstacles to proper yoga practice: lack of interest, doubt, laziness, sensuality, false knowledge, failure to concentrate, pain, despair, unsteadiness of body, sickness, and unsteadiness of respiration. Of these eleven obstacles only four have to do with the body. The rest are psychological, reflecting the disconnection of the mind, body and spirit.

Make a list now of your excuses – without censoring yourself. How does your list compare with the list above?

_____

_____

The excuse I hear the most is - I don't have time. Is it because we think we have to run the marathon or spend hours? In the beginning start off slowly, most of us can find time if it is just fifteen minutes each day. With the internet and cable channels and my home practice products, you can find time to meditate and do some exercising. Start slow and with easy exercises and just breathe for a few minutes a day then start to build upon that and soon you will be amazed that you are finding more time. The other most often used excuse is money...for this one I say it's all about priorities. If you want it bad enough you will find the money and again with the internet and all you don't really need much.

I allow my Physical Self to align with my Higher Self and release what no longer serves me, so I can accept the universe abundance!
--Melissa Stone

When you have listed your obstacles it is then easy to take a real look at it, eventually clearing the path. Perhaps removal of the obstacle will take a day or maybe months or just making the removal of that obstacle being your practice for now.

Notes:

_____

_____

_____

_____

Obstacles – Workbook six

<u>-Monday</u>
Make a list of all the things you have been trying to start and all your excuses.

_____   _____   _____

_____   _____   _____

_____   _____   _____

_____   _____   _____

<u>-Tuesday</u>
Take one item off the list and find fifteen minutes today to do it.

_____

<u>-Wednesday</u>
List other times in the day where you can spend fifteen minutes breathing or exercising.

_____   _____   _____

_____   _____   _____

-<u>Thursday</u>
Prioritize your spending. Are you spending currency on positive things?

_____   _____   _____

_____   _____   _____

How can you find money to do what you want, to get fit and eat right?

_____   _____   _____

_____   _____   _____

_____   _____   _____

_____   _____   _____

-<u>Friday</u>
Looking at your week did you eat right? If not how can you change this?

_____   _____   _____

_____   _____   _____

_____   _____   _____

_____   _____   _____

~ ॐ ~

Weekly Om – Seven

You – Is it Selfish to Be Good to You?

This one is my pet peeve, as I have had many lovers say to me that I am selfish for taking care of me in a situation. I needed to ponder this one long and hard; was I really being selfish to need to eat first, get some sleep or saying no I can't do that now?

Are you good to yourself? Do you feel it is selfish to give yourself what you want and need? Do you spend all your time pleasing others and depleting your own energy?

When you stop taking care of yourself, you will not be able to help others. You will become depleted and feel run down. Remember what is told to us when on an airplane, "Place the oxygen mask on yourself first!"

When you care about YOU, you then can care about others. This is not a selfish act! To be selfish means to look out for one's own interests, i.e. one's own life and no one else. To talk and act in ways that will only benefit you. I know that I want what is best for all in every situation and that putting boundaries, saying no and taking care of myself is not a selfish act. I now understand that being called selfish is just them projecting what they do not like about themselves onto me. I can see it and know and this will no longer affect me.

Taking care of you is necessary to be in balance. When you love you, you can participate in the world with unconditional love and support. When I cross paths with someone working in the emergency response profession I ask, "Are you taking care of yourself?" They all agree they could make more of an effort in taking care of themselves. I believe we all could do the same regardless of what we do for a living. I know that when I feel down, it is harder to love me. This is why we need support of family, friends and lovers that can remind us to love ourselves when we are down.

What does it mean to take care of yourself? It is basically giving to you what you need instead of getting it from outside. Listening and being in touch with your own physical body so that you will hear the signs of dis-ease or discomfort. It's like someone stepping on your foot you feel it, say "ouch" and they get off the foot. If you left that person on your foot for a longer period of time, you will have more dis-comfort and damage. If you continue to go

49

through life with someone stepping on your foot, life will be heavy, hard and uncomfortable. Get that person off your foot! Get in touch with your body, mind and spirit. And when you are stepping on others' feet... Listen to the "Ouch" and get off their foot! See the pain you are causing in others and be more compassionate. This is also giving of yourself. When we hurt others we are really hurting ourselves. When you hate, say bad things to others, or send others bad thoughts you are internally hurting yourself.

Negative thoughts and actions create negative energy all around us before it is sent off to them. It was made in our minds and flowed through our bodies first. Parts of that negative energy will stay in your body forever if you let it, causing its own pain and discomfort in you as well.

What are the body's needs? We all have been told for the body to function properly, it needs good nutrition, exercise, sleep and relaxation. Relaxation is the word we really do not understand... for some that means watching TV and others might think work is relaxing. Relaxation is the opposite of stress, the release of tension or the transition of state from a higher energy level to a lower one. If you really want to relax correctly you need to be working on transitioning the body's molecules from moving fast to moving slow. Recreational or leisurely activities might seem like they are relaxing but you still may be using your brain and moving in the high energy level state and watching TV is not relaxing to the body at all. Television, computers, iPods, and cell phones all have and release energy and light that over stimulate the molecules in the body. To truly relax you will need to slow down the breath to completely slow down these molecules and your body. This is where meditation or focusing on your breathing comes in and is needed to relax fully. When in this state you are giving yourself the healing that is needed to rejuvenate and reverse the discomfort and dis-ease.

Loving Yourself Meditation
Sitting in a comfortable place focusing on your Heart Chakra visualizing it as a lotus flower, as you inhale the petals open as you exhale the petals close. Focus on thinking about giving yourself peace and love as you inhale and as you exhale letting go of what limits you to loving yourself.

Notes:

_____

_____

_____

_____

You- Workbook seven

-<u>Monday</u>
Name five things you like to do for yourself but have not in a while.

_____   _____   _____

_____   _____

Do at least one on this list today.

-<u>Tuesday</u>
Make an appointment with yourself today for lunch, walk, shopping or to do something you enjoy.

-Wednesday
Pamper yourself tonight...take a hot bath (add in salts, oils and light candles), give yourself a facial, deep condition your hair, go to bed early without watching TV ....read a book or write about how you are feeling.

_____

_____

-Thursday
Look in the mirror and say, out loud: *"I love you!"*

Do this five times throughout the day. At the end of the day do the meditation and write down any differences in your mood energy or physical appearance

-Friday
Take yourself out to eat or to a movie or ask your family or roommates to leave you the house and rent a good movie and order take-out.

~ ॐ ~

Weekly Om – Eight

Self Esteem – Are You a Victim?

The root of our behavior is our beliefs. When we are feeling high self-esteem we believe in ourselves and our behavior will support a positive self. When we are feeling low self-esteem our behavior will demonstrate a negative self-concept. We condition ourselves to expect and assume certain things making our beliefs our habits. In order to change our habits we need to change our beliefs, when the beliefs change so then will our actions. However this takes time and practice. High self-esteem allows for the creative consciousness to become the belief and habit. Living in the creative consciousness is the state of mind that allows us to take control and to take the responsibility for our own destiny. On the other hand there is the victim consciousness state of mind that turns over all responsibility to someone or something else leaving us as the victim. We will blame others when we are in low self esteem or victim consciousness. Below are some examples of victim statements that I used in my earlier years.

- ~ I am afraid
- ~ You made me feel
- ~ It is their fault
- ~ No one cares

When we are thinking like this we are by definition a victim. We have given control over to someone or something else. If you feel that your life is not working then you are probably allowing yourself to be victimized. All decisions and actions are habits and come from your beliefs about yourself. Being the victim requires that we think we are not worthy and so we deserve to be manipulated by others.

Take back your power and stop being the victim!

A great way to make positive changes is the use of affirmations to change the habitual thought patterns.

Next time you look in the mirror say _"I am worthy of Love for myself"_.

Then keep reminding yourself every chance you get!

It's all just a journey. Let go of the control and accept it all.

Strive to move through the cycles of life with joy and acceptance, the acceptance of yourself.

Notes:

_____

_____

_____

_____

Self esteem – Workbook eight

-Monday
Write in three adjectives that you believe best describe you.

I am _____ _____

I am _____ _____

I am _____ _____

  ~ *Number them from 1 –3, with "1" being most important. Are these statements of your authentic self?*

What does that reveal about you? _____

Are you in high or low self-esteem? _____

-<u>Tuesday</u>

Look at your words from Monday if they are of low self-esteem. Look at it as if it were someone else and not you that you were describing. Would you be that judgmental or hard on them as you are on yourself? This is you remember. How would you feel if someone else described you this way?

If your words from Monday put you in high self-esteem, good for you!

You get to write down all the things you 'Should' do.

I Should _____

I Should _____

I Should _____

-<u>Wednesday</u>

If you did not do the 'I should' list, do it now.

Take each 'I Should' and read it out loud. Then add why you should.

Try to do it again and, end with *"because I really want to."*

I Should _____

I Should _____

I Should _____

-<u>Thursday</u>
Make a list of 'I Could', things that you really want to do but make excuses not to do.

I Could _____

I Could _____

I Could _____

Why have you not completed these things you want to do in your life? What stops you? Fear? Lack of self esteem? Motivation?

_____

-<u>Friday</u>
When you express your feeling you will feel less of that feeling. Express it now and let it go so you can feel it less. Keep expressing it until it diminishes. Meditate for thirty minutes on saying "*I am worthy.*"

~ॐ~

Self Discipline – How to Unleash Your Inner Strength

I am amazed and in awe of strong women, my mother being the strongest woman I know. The first woman I was amazed by was Mae West. She 'had it all' including not being afraid of her sex appeal.

We all have someone that we admire and respect. You might admire that they have the ability to learn something new or they are open to change. Maybe you have seen them overcome hardships. Why can't this be you? It actually can be you; all that is needed is learning how to tap into your own inner strength. We all have our lessons that we need to learn here on earth and we all have the potential to be strong. Your inner strength is the key to unlocking your lessons and learning how to get past them. We are all tested and tempted all day and every time we give in we are weakening our inner strength, along with weakening our bodies. Using the victim story is our way to justify the choices we make.

The potential is there right in the center of our being. We all have the strength inside to do anything we want and to help us get over anything we create. All you need is to find the key and unlock the door to unleash it. Starting an exercise plan today you will begin to strengthen your body and your muscles. When your body becomes strong then so will your mind.

Exercise is one way of strengthening the body and mind. Remember to use your core when holding these strong warrior poses.

The Warrior Series in Yoga

Warrior One – Standing in a lunge left leg forward right leg back (you may have the right knee down, if beginner) making sure the front knee does not bend past the toes. Exhale and sweep the arms over head clasping all but the pointer fingers. Holding straight lines with the body make sure to pull the navel into the spine and breathe. Try to hold for 30 seconds to start and work up to 2 minutes.
~Repeat on other side.

Warrior Two – Stepping feet wider than hips distance apart, point through left foot and pigeon the right toes in, arms out to the side, shoulders stacked on top of the hips. As you exhale bend through the left knee (pressing forward and back so the knee is over second toe). Hold for 30 seconds to start and work up to 2 minutes.
Repeat on other side.

Warrior Three – Standing with feet under hips aligning the arms with the ears. Exhale extending right leg back and lifting it up as you bring the arms with the torso down, balancing on the left leg. Hold for 30 seconds to start and work up to 2 minutes.
~Repeat on other side.

Meditations that focus on the Solar Plexus work well to create stronger energy within your body.

Pure Potential Meditation
~Focusing on the Solar Plexus located above the navel and below the breast bone
~Feeling this energy center that is your power and your will
~Seeing it emanating with yellow energy
~Feel the energy of your potential.... feel its power
~That power is always there waiting for you to use it
~See that there is no separation between you and this power!

Notes:

_____

_____

_____

_____

Self discipline – Workbook nine

~Monday

Inner strength is attained by overcoming inner resistance.
Find something you have been putting off (something that is easy to get done) and go do it. Don't let your laziness or the fact that you do not like to do that task, get the best of you. Take in a deep breath and muster up the energy to do the task.

How long did it take you to get the energy to do the task?   _____

How did you feel when that task finally was completed?   _____

~Tuesday

Get up thirty minutes early today and do the Warrior series before you start your day.
Make today the day you get the exercise you have wanted and need.
Remember <u>not</u> to listen to the excuses why you can't exercise today. It's only thirty minutes...YOU CAN DO IT!

How did you feel after you were done?   _____

-<u>Wednesday</u>
Do <u>not</u> listen to or create gossip today. Keep controlling your urges all day to speak about anything that is not important, only speaking about things that need talking about.

Did you speak less today?   _____

How did that feel?   _____

-<u>Thursday</u>
Take sugar and unhealthy food out of your diet today.

What did you turn down today? Make a list

_____   _____   _____

_____   _____   _____

_____   _____   _____

If you can turn it down today you can any other day. Keep it up.

-<u>Friday</u>
Clean out your drawers, closets and/or garage....get organized today and this weekend.
If you find yourself getting overwhelmed while doing this task.....take a break to meditate and while meditating see this task getting completed.

How did that feel to get organized?   _____

How long did it take to complete this task?   _____

~ ॐ ~

Inner Vision – How to Use Your Intuition to See Inward

I have been blessed with the ability to hear, see and feel my intuition. I am totally in my body and am able to change dis-ease before it gets out of control.

Are you in your body using your intuition to see the signs of dis-comfort? Do you feel that you are always with anxiety, stress or depression? That you are not living life fully as intended by your spirit?

Take this moment to notice where your body holds this tension. Do you hold your shoulders up and are they tight? Does your mid or lower back ache? Do you feel your heart racing or feel nervous energy like you can't sit still? These are early warning signs that we all need to listen to.

Listening in is just using your intuition, connecting the mind and body. When you use your intuition to listen to your body you can change and transform the dis-ease. Intuition can also be used to see what path you are on, to know if you are making the right choices. It is all inside of you: any dilemma you have or issue presented to you can be solved all by you using your intuition.

The sixth Chakra is the energy center for intuition it is called the Third Eye and is located in the mid forehead. The Third Eye is about seeing both internally and externally. In today's society we are always looking out of the body to fix things and make us happy.

What if you looked inward?

What would you see?

Since the Third Eye is located inside your head you cannot access it using physical exercises. Yoga and pranayama (breathing exercises) can be used as preparation for meditation as they help to calm down the mind and body. With meditation you can easily enter into the inner realms of the sixth Chakra.

Connecting with Intuition Meditation

Close your eyes and turn your awareness inward to the center of your forehead. It might help to take your index finger and hold that point until you can get it in focus. Feel the darkness and envision the dark blue color illuminating from the sixth Chakra, basking in this quite calm. Begin to make note of where you hold your stress. Is it in your feet, knees, hips, or legs? Abdomen, upper or lower back, how about your arms, shoulders and neck? Not to forget your face, eyes and ears. Now that you are aware of where you are holding the tension, as you inhale breathe in warmth and relaxation, and as you exhale breathe out the tension. Taking time and breathing until the tension is gone for each place that is holding. Then rub your hands together briskly until they are warm. Placing the palms over your eyelids feeling the warmth of energy and relax in the darkness. Returning yourself to the outside world as you open your eyes using your intuition now to free yourself from what limits you.

Notes:

_____

_____

_____

_____

Inner vision- Workbook ten

<u>-Monday</u>
After doing the meditation, what did you feel and see?

_____

_____

_____

<u>-Tuesday</u>
Wake up today and say out loud "I am going to listen to my intuition today."
And actually do it! Slow down and think before you talk and act today. Take
in a deep breath before getting frustrated, angry and stressed.

What did you notice?

_____

_____

_____

<u>-Wednesday</u>
Find at home or at your nearest crystal shop these stones:

--Lolite, Azurite, Angelite, Amethyst, Fluorite and Lapis Lazuli--

Wear them or carry them in your pocket today. Hold them in your palms
when doing the meditation.

<u>-Thursday</u>
Play a game of awakening intuition today -- when the phone rings think of who it is before you answer. Focus on the Third Eye, take a deep breath and do not peek.

How many times were you right?

_____

<u>-Friday</u>
Did you find you made better decisions, were less stressed or had clearer thoughts?

_____

What did you learn about yourself?

_____

_____

_____

~ ॐ ~

Anger – Where the Anger Begins

The two sensations of emotions that we possess are pleasure and pain. We do need to know pain and have it part of our lives to show the other side. To be in balance is to have the experience of both sides as there is always an opposite choice to make.

Anger begins in the Sacral Chakra (below the navel) as the emotion of hurt, guilt or fear. When these emotions are not expressed they are stored in the body, waiting for a time to be released. The more you store the angrier you will become when it's time to be released out. Or it will simply turn into pain or a disease. This is why anger is such a powerful emotion; it is held within your power house, your core, the center of your body. This is where your energy becomes potential and you are creating your reality from it. What reality are you creating if your energy is filled with anger?

You will store that energy there until you deal with it, feel it and release it. One day you might be too drained to keep it hidden within the body. Being depleted, tried and not in balance you release these emotions as anger. You say and take action of things you might regret later on anyone in your path. If you happen to be put in the presence of that same situation or person, the hurt just might return and come out as anger. This is generally the case in most abusive or violent relationships, letting this anger overcome you in an insignificant situation is easy when you are depleted and you are holding on to hurt feelings. If we had dealt with the hurt, guilt or fear when it happened, we would not have stored it. Then, when that 'insignificant situation' arose there would be no anger to bring up; things could have been made different just by letting out the feeling of hurt and feeling it at the time.

One way to let the hurt go is to communicate that hurt to the other person. If that cannot be done in a healthy fashion, you can let it go from your energy. You can use meditation, journaling or exercise to clear out these emotions with some time and work.

Hurt is felt in present time, and fear is felt when worrying about the future. Sometimes we redirect this hurt towards ourselves turning that hurt into negative self-talk, guilt and depression. Unexpressed anger redirected onto ourselves creates guilt. Depleting all your energy from negative self-talk and guilt could turn into a case of full-blown depression. Turning your life into this vicious cycle of anger and not knowing how to get out of it.

73

This is a tough place to be in! You can pull yourself out of it... by starting to use more positive ways to heal this past hurt. You do not even need to know what it is or where it came from. Just starting an exercise program and some bodywork will start to move the energy and past emotions out of the muscles. Start a meditation practice, taking fifteen minutes before you exercise to focus on the hurt and anger you might feel at times... asking it to leave freeing your body giving it new space for more peaceful and pleasant emotions.

Anger Meditation
~Start with Breathing Meditation to become relaxed.
~Take inventory in your body until you move to total relaxation.
~Create a symbol of your hurt guilt and anger.
~See it in your mind's eye, see it illuminated in red.
~Inhale; see your symbol in red, exhale see the red changing to light pink.
~See the anger becoming pink and changing now to a heart shape and feel the body relaxing.

Notes:

_____

_____

_____

_____

Anger – Workbook eleven

-Monday
If there has been hurt, guilt or worry in your home and your body, perform a 'cleanse' on yourself and your home today. Get a sage stick, burn it as you walk around filling each corner with the sage smoke, smudging. Say aloud – *"Letting anger go, I am Love, I give Love and I receive Love."*

Then smudge yourself with the sage sticks' ashes, and wave the sage sticks around you as you repeat the statement again.

-Tuesday
Make a list of what makes you angry. Go over the list and see if you are in control of anything on the list. Take the items of which you are in control and write out how you can change any or all of those situations.

_____   _____   _____

_____   _____   _____

_____   _____   _____

-Wednesday
On your list from yesterday - what can't you control? Do one of the energetic exercises to release the anger and let it go and the anger meditation, write about it in a journal or go for a run or exercise thinking about moving that energy out of your body.

_____   _____   _____

_____   _____   _____

-Thursday
Focus on being patient today with all and in every situation. Take in deep breaths when you feel frustration coming on. Walk away from a situation today let things cool down before you try to work something out with someone. If you had no situation that would have caused you anger save this one for a day when you do have a situation that brings on anger.

How did that work for you today? _____

_____

-Friday
Do something fearless today, even if it's small. Something you have been putting off doing because of being afraid.

What did you do and how did it make you feel?

_____

Grief – Are You Letting the Process Take Place?

I learned all about grief in 2004 when my semi-cousin Sergio Torros and my beloved friend Kathy Solari died four days apart from each other. I will talk more about these two in the Last Om Chapter.

Grief is a process and one that needs to happen in order to heal. There are different kinds of grief; the loss of someone close to you, a crime, health issues or anything that causes a change in life can cause grief.

Everyone handles their grief in different ways but pushing it away and not feeling it is not the best solution. By not feeling the grief, you are hurting yourself in many ways. When you are storing this sadness and sorrow in the body, letting it sit there will cause it to manifest into health problems, depression or addiction. It can be painful to feel your grief but is a natural and a necessary process for working through it. Thinking about the consequences, isn't it better to feel the grief as an emotion at the time, work through it, and then get back to living life? Or would you rather feel it as an ongoing physical pain or even becoming seriously ill later in life, when you could be pain free and happy?

The grief process is one that cannot be rushed, be patient with yourself using the tools of coping. Create a support system for your grief; see a counselor or surround yourself with others that allow you to go through your process without judgment or without adding more to your load. Take care of yourself; let the others take care of themselves, so that you can focus on helping you get through this time.

Using positive self talk, making good nutrition choices and taking time for exercise and meditation is key in this time of need.

It is okay to cry and let others see you being sad. In this society we are told to be strong and not show these emotions, especially men. Being sad and recognizing a loss by crying is a total cleansing process that is needed by the body. When you feel the need to cry let it flow, stop being embarrassed or think others will judge you for it. If you need it give it to yourself. If you have a dog or cat let them love you while you cry, animals are great at comforting their owners.

Last but not least, wrap your arms around your shoulders and just give yourself a hug. You are wonderful and worthy of your own love!

If you are grieving a loved one make sure to read the chapter on death because death is not the end, it is the beginning of a wonderful journey for your loved one. A journey that we will all be on some day, they are not gone as they are energetically still here if you open yourself up to feeling them.

If it is a life change you are grieving, maybe try to open yourself up to that change -- saying to yourself *"This moment is the way it should be."* Then believe it, because it is true each moment is as it should be. If the change is not one you are wanting then use meditation to create what you want and remove the grief from your life. Try to flow with the change instead of against it.

Notes:

_____

_____

_____

_____

Grief – Workbook twelve

~Monday
Make of list of the things you are grieving. Give yourself the gift of a good cry.

_____   _____   _____

_____   _____   _____

_____   _____   _____

_____   _____   _____

~Tuesday
If you are grieving someone's passing write a letter to him or her, plant a tree in their honor or 'take a walk down memory lane' by looking at photos or that person's mementos.

~Wednesday
Sit in a comfortable position focusing on your breathing. Think about what you are grieving, focus on it. Is it something that is in your control? If you could let it go would you feel better? See the person, situation or thing in your mind's eye and as you exhale see it floating away. Journal your experience or feel it by letting yourself cry. It is okay to cry it is beneficial to our body's chemistry.

_____

_____

<u>-Thursday</u>
Find an affirmation(s) that fit your situation and place them all around you. Repeat them out loud when you see them at least three times.

_____

_____

_____

<u>-Friday</u>
End any turmoil with those close to you, using the tool of forgiveness. Write letters to them forgiving them of the actions and situations that keep you both in turmoil. If appropriate mail the letter to them. If not, burn the letter as you send them love and understanding through your thoughts.

~ ॐ ~

Fear – Why you Should Let It Go

To live in fear is what holds us back from becoming our authentic self and to heed our calling in this life. It stops you from enjoying life, from having freedom and being at peace.

It closes you off from having the experience of what you are afraid of. Fear is only...

F - False
E- Emotions
A- Appearing
R- Real

It is the feeling of dread caused by your own controlling thoughts of worry. Wasting precious time over the unknown and only looking at the negative side until you are fearful and talking yourself out of what scares you. When you let go of fear many doors will open.

Through meditation, the quieting of the mind, you will start the connection to really look at life and what your fears might be. Maybe you will start to recognize when the universe hands you opportunities in order to set you up on your path of dreams. When you see situations as opportunities knocking, you then gladly go with the attitude of a fearless and confident spirit.

The universe rewards us with everything we ask for and all it wants in return is for us to appreciate what we already have and walk our path in truth.

Sounds easy? No, it is the ultimate challenge. We are human and want the magic pill or the easy way out instead. If you continue to push against the universe and the laws of attraction your life will always feel like a struggle.

Our patterns, past experiences and environment keep us in fear. The biggest fear is the fear of change which is the first step. The only way to bring in something new into your life is to change your surroundings, your habits and your situations. To let go of something in order for there to be room to bring in what you want.

It all starts with recognizing that you are living in fear and with fear. Then just start to do good things for yourself that will help you to let FEAR go.

I am willing to create my reality releasing my fear as I resonate with love!
--Unknown

~ Meditation
~ Exercising
~ Body work
~ Eating healthy
~ Loving yourself enough (you are worth it)

Notes:

_____

_____

_____

_____

Fear – Workbook thirteen

<u>~Monday</u>
Be honest and list all of your fears. Why do you think you have each of these fears?

_____   _____   _____

_____   _____   _____

_____   _____   _____

<u>~Tuesday</u>
Go to the beach and write your fears in the sand ~~ and let the water wash them all away.

<u>~Wednesday</u>
Copy your list and ask for spirits to help in transforming the fear into positive energy and then set the paper on fire, transforming your fear as they burn.

_____   _____   _____

_____   _____   _____

_____   _____   _____

<u>-Thursday</u>

Take one fear at a time and list out action plans to overcome the fears. Do not let money, or time, be excuses. Make plans for a future date and put it on your calendar to work out the action that it would take to overcome this fear. It might be doing something small everyday or often, whatever it is make the plan(s) now.

_____   _____   _____

_____

_____

_____

_____   _____   _____

_____

_____

_____

_____   _____   _____

_____

_____

_____

-<u>Friday</u>
Meditate one by one on your list of fears.

See each fear as a symbol and see the cord attaching it to you.

Take a deep breath and on the exhale cut that cord and see it falling far away.

~ ॐ ~

Weekly Om – Fourteen

Envy – Is It Worth Losing Your Higher Power?

Envy is an emotion that occurs when a person thinks they lack another's superior quality or gift. Not at all recognizing his/her own potential. They spend all their energy on being in this envious state, wasting precious moments of time.

Hatred is also part of the emotion of envy. Knowing no gratitude is an emotion that will lead to a person unable to be pacified. These are the traits of envy. Envy creates a person of weak mindedness and of self -loathing.

When you are in envy you cannot see your blessings, always wanting what the others have instead of looking at what you have. Ignoring your own blessings keeps you stuck and stops your own spiritual growth. Envy is associated with greed and desires for material wealth. It spins your world out of control when greed and envy are your emotions, causing pain for yourself and others. Just look at what being greedy has done for our government. This is not a political statement, only my opinion. I am sure you all know a greedy person or company and can see what I am trying to explain.

If we could all focus on our blessings and how to help and bless others we would be provided for and have all that we want. There is no need for the emotions of greed, envy or hatred. They are all a waste of precious time, because there is enough for us all here on earth.

Clearing Envy Meditation
Sit in a comfortable position and take in three deep breaths, let the rib cage open feeling the heart lift up in the center of your chest. Think of someone or something that you now envy. Visualize one thing that you envy and then see how you could have it as well; feel it becoming your new focus and how you can go about getting it or if you really want it at all. Send love and kindness to those that you have envied in the past and let the old stuff go.

Notes:

_____

_____

_____

_____

Envy – Workbook fourteen

<u>-Monday</u>
Make a list of everything that you envy, all that you have greed for and everything you hate.

_____   _____   _____

_____   _____   _____

_____   _____   _____

~ Say "I *love you*" to everything on this list, post the list where you can see it every day.

I open my heart to love and kindness as I let the envy leave my Mind, Body and Spirit.
-Unknown

<u>-Tuesday</u>
Say 'I love you' to everything on this list, and do the meditation above.

92

-Wednesday
Say 'I love you' to everything on this list, and do the meditation above.

-Thursday
Do you love them yet? If not spend more time tonight repeating the above.

-Friday
How have you changed? If in no ways, then keep doing this exercise every day until you see one.

When someone tells you good news, have joy for them and not envy. Practice this once every day.

_____   _____   _____

~ ॐ ~

Jealousy - Where Is Your Self Worth?

Jealousy is the feeling of resentment towards someone or something that threatens us or makes us feel less of. It is an emotion that takes control, wastes precious time and wrecks lives. Being jealous is again being in fear. What is a fear? 'A False Emotion Appearing Real.'

If jealousy were tangible and had a shape, it would be the shape of a boomerang. The only person that is hurt by jealousy is you, it will always come back to hurt you. The other party probably does not even feel or know your pain. This is another emotion that is made up by your ego because of low self worth.

Denial of jealously will just keep it stored inside. It's a powerful ugly emotion that will eat away your authentic soul. Dealing with the jealousy will create pain, but it is the only way to rid yourself of it. When working on ridding yourself of this powerful emotion, be sure you are not transforming the jealousy into actions of bad intentions. Jealousy becomes anger in a furious way and can be very destructive. It has made some hurt others in many ways including taking lives.

Your healing will begin when you start to become aware of how you and your relationships and situations are being affected by jealous thoughts, words and actions. Maybe letting go of those that leave you feeling jealous is the answer or realizing that you do not have the power to control others. Mostly it's about knowing that you are unique and finding what your gifts are so that you can love you just the way you are and stop wanting what others have.

God grant me the serenity to accept the things I cannot change; courage to change the things I can; and the wisdom to know the difference.
-- Reinhold Niebuhr

The Serenity Prayer is best in situations of not being in control.

Say this prayer while looking at the jealously you are feeling. Is it a valid emotion in this situation? Focus on pulling up some energy from your

95

Solar Plexus, giving yourself back some self worth and getting out of the situation that brings on the thoughts of being jealous.

Notes:

_____

_____

_____

_____

Jealousy – Workbook fifteen

-<u>Monday</u>
Think of a situation that makes you feel jealous. Write about why you feel this way? Be honest with yourself.

_____

_____

_____

_____

~   Is it valid? Can you let go of the control?

-<u>Tuesday</u>
Make a list of all your jealous feelings and who they are toward or about.

Close your eyes and focus on clearing this energy from your thoughts and body.

Write about how that felt.

_____   _____   _____

_____   _____   _____

_____   _____   _____

_____

_____

-<u>Wednesday</u>
Pick one of the situations that make you feel jealous. Why do you feel this way?
Could it be lack of self-esteem? What action can you take to overcome this feeling for this situation? How do you feel after looking at it and creating action to dissolve it?

_____

_____

_____

-<u>Thursday</u>
Pick another and answer the same questions.

_____

_____

-<u>Friday</u>
Now focus on you and finding the seeds of your jealousy inside you, clear the old voices and experiences. Put all the energy into building your personal and emotional security.

~ ॐ ~

Weekly Om – Sixteen

Stress –What Does Ego Have to Do With it?

Looking back I was one stressed out person, trying to control it all and storing it all in my body. I would attend stress workshops where they would help me see that I was stressed out but would never tell me how to get out of the stress. I finally realized that I gave myself most of the stress by not speaking my truth and giving myself a hard time if something was not met. I made up my own unrealistic deadlines to try to control my world and I was not being kind to myself.

It is natural to have a certain amount of tension in the living process we call life. When life is in its flow we are spontaneous, confident, courageous and centered, but when experiencing stress we tend to be self-conscious and full of doubt. Along with the emotional turmoil we put ourselves through come physical symptoms such as high blood pressure, chronic headaches, irritable bowel syndrome, and ulcers.

Understanding that the stress is really nothing but a mismanagement of our time and energy is necessary to release stress. Instead of living in the present we are worried and reducing our available time for the present, thus bringing on more worries about not having enough time to do what you want to accomplish.

These worries and not being in the present moment will cause a vicious cycle for us to be less efficient in dealing with life's tasks and problems. Locking us in and stressing us out. Our sleep may become affected and then more irritableness and bad eating habits may begin. Sugar is then craved and addiction to alcohol might begin.

From a philosophical point of view, stress can be characterized as a state of ego. The ego feels it does not have enough time to express itself. It fears its own demise and tries to suck up every drop of time; leaving our search for happiness and fulfillment in more of a frustrated mood. Transcend the ego and leave behind the stress. Stop clinging to a limited sense of who you are or are not.

Letting go of ego and letting in a sense of being. Being present, being in the moment and breathing will transcend the stress and help you to relax. Yoga and meditation help through relaxation of the mind transcending the ego where it lives. Each time you move to relaxation instead of stressing out, you bring the ego to a deeper level of relaxation. This opens up spirit and brings you closer to being in the present moment. Yogic concentration leads to meditation and meditation is the ground from which the seed of super conscious ecstasy, present in all of us, may burst out in full flower. Letting life become a playful drama in which we can joyfully participate without stress.

Letting Go of Stress: Breathing
-Start breathing from the belly....
-Inhale in through the nose all the way down to the bottom of the belly; count to five as you inhale, let the belly rise and hold the breath.
-Exhale out let the belly fall on the count of five.
-Take in as many breaths as you need to move to relaxation.

Letting Go of Stress: Meditation
-Start with Breathing Meditation and become relaxed.
-Take inventory in your body until you move to total relaxation.
-Create a symbol of your stress, situation or person.
-See it in your mind's eye; see a cord attaching it to you like a balloon.
-Inhale see it, exhale cut the cord and release it.
-See the stress floating away and feel the body relaxing.
-If it is something you need to pick back up later, like work.
-Then tie the balloon to a tree on the way home from work and pick it back up the next day.

<u>Notes:</u>

_____

_____

_____

Stress – Workbook sixteen

-Monday
Do some breathing today before you start the day for at least fifteen minutes.

Use this breathing throughout the day when you feel stressed.

Find a tree, rock or fence on the way home from work for you to hang your work stress and deadlines on, leave them there and pick them back up on the way to work the next day.

-Tuesday
Belly breathe all day.
Make a list of what stresses you out and why. Make notes; are these things within your control? Are they things that need to be in your life? Or do they no longer serve you?

_____ _____ _____

_____ _____ _____

-Wednesday
Belly breathe all day.
Look again at your notes find the items that are no longer serving you.
Write down what these items are and how your life would change if you released them only list positives.

_____ _____ _____

_____ _____ _____

_____

_____

-Thursday
Belly Breathe all day
Take your list of no longer needed items and closing your eyes think about it in your mind's eye. See a cord attaching it to you and take a deep breath and release it say, I love you, but goodbye to each item on your list. Be as creative as you want in the way to see them fall away.

_____ _____ _____

_____ _____ _____

-Friday
Write about how you are feeling, when thinking about these items now. Notice that your breathing is it different? Keep up the breathing every day and when stressed.

_____

_____

_____

_____

_____

~ ॐ ~

Weekly Om – Seventeen

Lotus of Unconditional Love – What is The Heart Chakra

I learned what unconditional love is, fully, when I was in massage school. To give a healing massage to someone you have to be able to tap into this place in your heart. To give this type of love you need to let go of judging others and to just be in a place of love. I am honored to be able to give this to anyone that is in need of healing. Thinking about dogs especially my dog Max, they can give love so unconditionally. Learn from your dog and give that love to yourself first, then to all others.

Unconditional Love.....What does it mean?
Webster's Dictionary defines it as "not limited in any way".
What really limits us from having and giving this kind of Love?

These past weeks we have gone over the type of emotions that block our energy - that they are negative emotions. The human body is an amazing force of energy flowing in many different directions. One cooperative network of energy fields is known as the Chakras. This is a Sanskrit word meaning "spinning wheel". Chakras can be described as spinning vortexes of activity created by the presence of consciousness within the physical body. These vortexes exist within what is called the subtle body (aura), a hidden field of energy that carries your urges, emotions and habits and imprints them into your aura, a collection of energy that is all that has happened in your life.

The Heart Chakra is the fourth of the seven. It is the energy center for unconditional love for yourself and for others and is located in the center of your chest. When it is in balance it allows us to love, trust, and feel deep compassion for others. When imbalanced these qualities can become twisted, leading us to feeling hate, fear, jealously. Blockages here can also manifest as an imbalance in the immune system and disease in the cardiovascular system because of its relation to the physical heart, the circulatory system and the blood. When existing without the positive influence of the fourth Chakra you may feel disconnected, isolated, and

I live love, I give love,
I am love.
-- Melissa Stone

filled with unexpressed emotions. Too much Heart Chakra influence can lead to restlessness, dreaminess, and aimless wandering.

There are many ways to rebalance your Heart Chakra or heart center. The easiest of influence is to remember to love yourself without limits and to learn to laugh often and freely. Other ways to influence the change in your body and in your Chakras is to meditate with some breathing and visualization techniques.

Opening Up the Heart Chakra Meditation

Sitting in a comfortable position or lying down with your arms at your side palms up, focus on breathing from the belly but also into the heart center. Feel the chest soften as you breathe. Now visualize the heart as a lotus flower and inhale the petals open and exhale the petals closed. Try adding color; the Heart Chakra is the color of green.

Visualize the heart glowing with green energy as you breathe in opening the petals, and out closing the petals. Green energy is healing energy; see the green energy flowing throughout the body.

I like to do this type of meditation lying in bed before I get up in the morning or before I fall asleep. You can take one minute or you can take fifteen. It's up to you. The Heart Chakra is the point of new beginnings. Nurture it, and you will find that contentment will emerge from all aspects of your being and your life.

There is no exercise better for the heart than
reaching down and lifting people up ... and
see what such a day would bring to you.
--Edgar Cayce

Notes:

_____

_____

_____

_____

Lotus of unconditional love – Workbook seventeen

-<u>Monday</u>
Do the meditation before you start this week of practicing unconditional love. Then practice random acts of kindness all day.

-<u>Tuesday</u>
Think of a friend or family member who is difficult, but whom you love anyway. See how you show unconditional love in that relationship anyway but still can see the difficulty of the person. Use that as an example to every other difficult person that crosses your path today and every day.

-<u>Wednesday</u>
Apologize to someone today, some old situation or maybe you lost your temper yesterday at the store clerk. Make it a point to say I am sorry and thank you for the lesson, then let it go.

-<u>Thursday</u>
Has anyone noticed you are being kinder? If so, good for you! If not, do the meditation longer, and give more.

_____

-<u>Friday</u>
Practice loving-kindness for all beings. Do this going forward forever.

~ ॐ ~

Transforming Hatred into Love - How to Love What You Hate

It takes a lot of energy to hate. It has a great impact on the person who hates but at the same time sends negative energy to all around the situation. It keeps you stuck in negativity. Yet overcoming hatred is difficult because it keeps reinforcing itself and causes ill will to come into being.

When you practice loving what you hate you start to create profound changes in your emotions and your life. You will see the changes happening quickly if you keep saying I love it instead of I hate it. At first it may feel like a lie but keep doing it and you will notice you might even really love it. It is truly a difficult task to forgo judging someone, loving your enemy and seeking good positive situations for yourself and others. But each time you do decide to Love What You Hate you become one less person putting negativity out into the world.

What if we all decided to stop using hate as our excuse, purpose or pleasure? Would we have world peace? Would there then be enough? I think so!

Wars are started with hate.
Peace begins with love,
You decide which is better.
--Melissa Stone

Empower yourself today by loving something you thought you hated and see that you probably made it all up and really don't hate it at all.

Transforming Hate Into Love Meditation

Sit in a comfortable position, closing your eyes breathing from your belly focusing your awareness in the Heart Chakra (center of the chest). Feeling the heart center soften and visualizing it growing larger with each breath. Think of something, someone or a situation that you feel like you hate and visualizing surrounding it with white light and love. If you start to feel uneasy or stressed see a thin white thread that attaches it to you and cut it. This will symbolize letting go of the emotion. Then go back to surrounding it with the white light until you feel like the hate has turned into love. End with surrounding yourself with white light feeling this same love for yourself.

Notes:

_____

_____

_____

_____

Transforming hatred into love – Workbook eighteen

-Monday

~ Stop your negativity all day today, instead of saying "I hate" say "I love".

~ Instead of giving negative gestures at people when mad give the peace sign. Sending others love all day when they are difficult with you, will transform hate into love.

~ Instead see the pain that keeps them difficult. It's not you it's them...so don't be like them!

-<u>Tuesday</u>
Make a list of things you hate to do at work and decide to love them instead.
Do at least two of the tasks on your list with a smile on your face and loving
each moment.

_____   _____   _____

_____   _____   _____

How long did it take you to complete each task? What did you notice?

_____   _____   _____

_____   _____   _____

-<u>Wednesday</u>
Make a list of things that you need to get done around the house but hate to
do.

_____   _____   _____

_____   _____   _____

Take a big project on the list and break it up into small parts and schedule in
time all week to work on it. Note how you feel at the end of the project about
getting it done.

<u>-Thursday</u>
We spend more time at work than at home.

Do you really love what you spend your time doing? If not, take some time today to meditate on what you would love to do. Write what you felt or see.

_____

_____

_____

_____

<u>-Friday</u>
Keep working on this doing the meditations, your lists at home and at work, and with all the difficult people in your life.

~ ॐ ~

Living Creatures - How the Pieces Fit

We are drawn to people of our own like energy and to those that are here to help or teach us. Living beings, however long they are in our lives, are in them to make some kind of contribution.

I cannot think of anyone that I have known that has not taught me something or helped me in one way or another. Looking back I can see where knowing one person lead me to another and so on. I feel life is a big huge puzzle and we are all the pieces putting us all together making "One Love." When the puzzle piece does not fit we tend to try to force it. We use all our energy but can't make that person or situation fit with ease and peace.

When one door closes another door opens.
-- Alexander Graham Bell

Whether in a game or in reality, that piece just will not fit, it's better to release that person or situation. Letting go will allow the will of the universe to do its work bringing balance.

I have been through a large number of layoffs in my lifetime career and I have always found the above quote from Alexander Graham Bell to be true. This is also true when I let go of a relationship with a friend or lover. It is a hard one to remember in the time of need, so place this statement somewhere so you will trust it and know it for sure. Don't ever feel that a negative relationship or job was a waste of time as it was not at all; it just took you a little while to realize the lesson.

We may also know each other from past lives; maybe we did not learn or teach the lesson the first time so we are here again trying to figure it out. Whatever the situation is; it is clear it's all for a reason and all for the bigger picture. Only the Divine knows so let it flow.

Expect nothing, appreciate everything.
-- Unknown

Taking time now to look at all that is present in your life and appreciating <u>all</u> living creatures for the gifts and lessons that they bring to us.

Notes:

_____

_____

_____

Living Creatures – Workbook nineteen

-Monday
Hug someone today that you would not normally hug and smile at everyone.

-Tuesday
Do some people watching today; notice how others interact with each other. Is it loving and kind? What did you notice? Would you change anything you saw?

_____

_____

-Wednesday
Make a list of everyone you appreciate and why. Starting today make it a point to tell them.

_____   _____   _____

_____   _____   _____

_____   _____   _____

-<u>Thursday</u>
Start today off with no expectations and give appreciation to all beings.
Was this easy or hard?

_____   _____   _____

_____   _____   _____

-<u>Friday</u>
Think about people that have come and gone in your life and see if you can
notice reasons or lessons behind their arrival and departure. Start to notice
how you are in others lives for a reason or a lesson. Make a list if you want or
write out how all the puzzle pieces fit.

_____

_____

_____

_____

~ ॐ ~

Weekly Om – Twenty

Wild Wisdom – What Can We Learn From Animals?

On our journey to enlightenment we can learn much from our companions.

Take for example your house pet, how they love unconditionally. Not caring about our size, shape, gender or race they just enjoy loving and being loved. There are many lessons we can learn from animals from our house pets to animals out in the wild and even insects.

Unlike humans, animals can only impact us with their wisdom by example as we learn by observation. Animals teach us about behavior, habit, and instinct.

Our pets teach us about letting our guard down, being playful and enjoying life. About being happy to see the ones they love when they have been away. My dog is a great teacher of compassion, he knows when I am down and always comes to me and puts his head in my lap to say 'I love you!'

Animals in the wild can teach you how to let go, as they shake out their negative emotions. When an animal in the wild feels pain or has a negative situation, they instinctively start to do large belly breaths and shake out the negative situation so they can be free of the negativity.

They also can teach us how to adapt to one's environment. Animals that live in rivers, oceans and lakes can teach us the value of movement and grace. They can teach us about life, death, sacrifice, and responsibility.

Take some time today to watch an animal be in nature as it gathers its food or runs about playing and enjoying life.

The other day I parked in my driveway and looked at the electrical line to the house. There were two grey doves sitting but because they both were on the line they had to flip flop their tails to stay in balance. Ones tail would go up and the other down working together to stay in balance on the wire. I watched this with such joy for about five minutes then they flew away. I was thinking while watching how in relationship both need to work for it to stay in balance. One is up when the other is down with both helping each other to stay on the wire. I love to watch animals as a relaxing hobby, because it helps to put all things in perspective, as animals are pure spirit in physical form.

Wild Wisdom – Workbook twenty

-<u>Monday</u>
If you have a pet, watch him or her play. Take some time today to play with them or just sit quietly with them petting them and talking to them. How calm does this make you feel? If you do not have pets, why not look into getting one? If you cannot have any make a donation to your closest animal shelter.

---   ---   ---

-<u>Tuesday</u>
Find some time today to gaze out the window at a bird, squirrel or your own pet. If none around you go to a park or the beach and watch the animals play and frolic. Ask yourself which of their/its traits you find most intriguing and think about how you might mimic those traits within your own life.

---   ---   ---

-Wednesday

Write about what you learned from watching the animals play. Keep learning about animals; even watch animal shows on TV.

_____

_____

_____

-Thursday

Take your dog to a new place or for a ride, get your cat, bird or fish a new toy. If you do not have a pet buy a treat for a friend's pet.

-Friday

Rent a movie with animals in it. Take your pet out to play then sit and watch the movie as if they are enjoying it as well.

~ ॐ ~

Breathing or Pranayama - How are you breathing?

It is obvious that we need to breathe to subsist. Yet no one teaches us about breathing and we do it without any thought. Most of us are breathing incorrectly and if we just focused on our breathing we might be able to change our energy, emotions and our life. We breathe roughly 23,000 times a day and take in about 4,500 gallons of air and 25 times that amount during exercise. Now can you see the importance of the breath? No wonder it profoundly influences our health, body and mind.

Breathing is not just a physical process; it is also closely connected with the functioning of the mind and emotions. Notice when you get upset, agitated or depressed, or when you get overly excited or happy; how your breathing patterns change. When the breathing rhythms change the state of mind and emotions are affected. The fact is if you regularize your breathing patterns your thoughts and emotions will become stabilized as well, allowing a more relaxed and at-ease body and mind.

Along with noticing your breathing patterns, you should also notice how much of the diaphragm you use and how much oxygen you are taking in. Are you allowing the diaphragm to expand fully and bring in enough oxygen to feed the body? There are three types of breathers: nasal, chest and belly.

~ Nasal breathers are not using the diaphragm at all to breathe, leaving that organ sitting stagnant and are not bringing enough oxygen into the body.
~ Chest breathers are only using half of the diaphragm to breathe, bringing in some oxygen but still not enough.
~ The belly breathers are using the full diaphragm to breathe and are bringing in enough oxygen to feed the body.

You can be one of these types or all three at times. It is best to be a belly breather all the time; keeping the breathing rhythm at a smooth slow pace. This allows you to be calm and at peace. The way to tell how you breathe is by lying down and putting your hands on your belly. You are taking normal breaths if

Be grateful for your breath and the ability to breathe.
--Melissa Stone

your belly is rising (becoming full) as you inhale and falling as you exhale. If your chest rises and falls you are breathing into your chest and need to work on bringing each breath down to the full diaphragm. If neither the belly nor the chest rise and fall you are breathing from your nasal cavity and really need to start working on bringing the breath down through the diaphragm. Remember breathing is our Life Force energy, our chi and is so important for that mind, body and spirit connection.

Breathing Meditation

Use when you need to relax or to bring yourself back into your body and to become aware of your breathing. You can do this sitting, standing or lying down. Inhale through the nose all the way down to the bottom of the belly. Let the belly rise, and exhale out through parted lips - making a 'HA' sound by constricting through the throat while the belly falls. Take in as many breaths as you need to move to relaxation.

Notes:

_____

_____

_____

_____

Breathing or Pranayama - Workbook twenty one

-Monday
Do fifteen minutes of belly breathing today. Did you notice a difference in your body today?

_____

-Tuesday
Do twenty-five minutes of belly breathing today. Did you notice a difference in your body today?

_____

-Wednesday
Do thirty minutes of belly breathing today. Did you notice a difference in your body today?

_____

-Thursday
Start to add the belly breathing in when faced with stress throughout the day.

Keep up the thirty minutes of breathing even if you need to split it up and do fifteen in the AM and fifteen in the PM.

-Friday
How has your stress level changed? Are you noticing when stressed that you start to do the belly breathing on your own? If not, keep up the breathing meditation for thirty minutes a day until you do.

_____

_____

~ ॐ ~

Movement and Breathing - How Are You Moving With Each Breath?

Last week's Om was about how we breathe. This week I would like to share information I have learned about movement and breath. Breathing directly affects both external and internal movement. It is the biggest influence in shaping the posture.

In the Hatha Yoga practice the posture and your breathing is the most important structure. When you are in deep breathing patterns the movement begins from the deeper regions of the body, and then travels outward and up the spine. By using our physical movement with the breath we gain both internal and external benefits. We maximize the effect of each movement of the spinal column, the tissues and the organs of the body.

The following are movements that you can use to practice in unison with the breath. Practice the movement while taking long deep breaths using the belly breathing. Make each movement as you breathe.

~ Forward Bending occurs more easily during the exhalation. Start in Mt Pose- standing lifting through the breast bone inhaling the arms up to the sky, exhaling rotating the hips forward, palms to the floor, forward bending block or holding opposite elbows. Repeat three to five times

~ Movements that expand the chest are initiated during inhalation. Lie on the front body, hands outside the breast bone, inhale rolling the chest up and open the shoulders wide as you lift, exhale as you move back to floor. Repeat three times "

~ When the core (abdominal area) is being compressed using an exhalation is best. Moving to the sit bones extending the legs out inhale lifting up through the breast bone, exhaling folding forward, palms on legs or feet. Repeat three times

~ You will move farther during the exhalation for twisting movements Lying on your back, knees bent legs in table top exhale as you twist the legs to the left side, inhale center then exhale right side Repeat three times both sides.

~ Backward Bending is executed better during inhalation. Lying on your back knees bent feet on the floor, inhale as you roll the tail bone off the floor and roll all the way up to the shoulders, exhale as you roll back down one vertebra at a time. Repeat three to five times.

131

Practicing these movements for just fifteen minutes each day will not only give you some exercise, it will help you to become flexible and teach you how to choreograph the breath to your movements. You will then find yourself dancing through life.

Notes:

_____

_____

_____

_____

Movement and Breathing- Workbook twenty two

-Monday
Be aware of your breath and movement all week

Do the breathing and movement exercises for fifteen minutes today.

-Tuesday
Notice how you are breathing all day today when making any twisting movements throughout the day.

-Wednesday
The forward bend movements restore the body's energy so use this today when you feel you need to restore yourself then notice how you are breathing.

Thursday
Do you notice a change in your awareness of your breathing and movements?

Write about it...what has changed? Are you more relaxed and at ease?

_____

_____

_____

-Friday
Do the breathing and movement exercises for thirty minutes today.

~ ॐ ~

Ether Element – Are You Aware Of the Space Around You?

The highest of elements is called Ether and is also considered the element of unconditional love. This element is the closest to us. It is around us and fills us; it is the region of all space. Ether holds all forms and colors; it is the base of all sounds. It is the source of energy from which all else flows, running from head to toe.

I believe the Ether Element is God. Please do not take this as religion because it is only Spirituality I talk about. But when Jesus said, "The kingdom of God is within you", I believe he is referring to the Ether Element. God is not sitting in a chair somewhere way up in the sky. He/she is what flows all around us and through us all at all times. It is what we breathe into our bodies this source of power our life force energy. This element is the creator of it all.

Ether's instrument is the human body, becoming a proper instrument when we open up space for the ether to fill in order to create our own power from it. When we are full of the Ether we can do great things. All things thought of that are in alignment with good will manifest. I have seen it happen over and over again in my life. I will say something or think one thing and boom I am being offered it with little or no effort.

Cleansing out all emotional blockages will help you to become aware of wisdom from the Spirit and the Heavens. When you are in awareness and full of ether you will feel ecstasy, illumination, fearlessness, rapture, joy and revelation.

The awareness will not happen if you are filled up with stress, workload and worries.

These negative feelings keep you locked up in fear and the source power that you then breathe in is not enough to keep the body running much less connect you with the spirit so you can hear the wisdom.

I follow my joy to abundance, prosperity and fulfillment.
--Unknown

Filling Up With Ether Meditation

Finding a quite place and sitting in a comfortable position. Focus on your breathing, feeling the body relaxing with each deep breath. Give Ether the color of gold and see it start to rain upon you with its golden light. Open up the Crown Chakra, at the top of the head and fill yourself with the divine energy of Ether. See the golden light fill you up, just like filling up a cup of water. Feel yourself becoming fearless and illuminating with joy. Stay here as long as you can, and feel the unconditional love of the universe.

Notes:

_____

_____

_____

Ether Element – Workbook twenty three

-Monday

Find a spot at lunch outside and watch the sky, see the clouds move making pictures and smell the air. What did you see and smell.

_____

-Tuesday

Sit outside either before you start or day or at the end as long as it takes to feel the stillness and love that fills the air. What did you feel?

_____

136

-Wednesday
Notice the ether element at work in your life. Notice unconditional love today.

Write or think about what it was and how it made you feel.

_____

_____

-Thursday
While sitting outside today focus on opening up and letting in the ether element feeling -- letting it flow all around and through you. What did you feel?

_____

-Friday
Make a list of what fills your body, sit outside letting the ether fill you and see if you can think of what now fills you that you would like to let go of in order to have more ether flowing through you.

_____ _____ _____

_____ _____ _____

~ ॐ ~

Weekly Om – Twenty Four

Air Element – Are You Breathing?

The Air Element is my favorite out of the five elements, it is said this element represents our thoughts and mental clarity. It is close to being Ether. It is not seen, but a force that is most effective, it governs our spirit and is the force that lives in all of us... as our breath or chi.

We should all see the element of Air as Universal Power, a pure substance. It's of fundamental importance to life; such words as spirit, inspire, and aspire are derived from the Latin word *spirare* ("to breathe").

Using the breath to cleanse the body just as Mother Nature uses the wind to cleanse the earth. Air, Wind or Breath are all elements that create a cleansing on an energetic level as they clear out old stagnant energy to make space for new energy.

Sit quietly outside during the next windy day and focus on only the wind, feeling it flow though you and around you. If you focus long enough you can hear the spirits whispering information and guidance to your consciousness.

I remember as a kid how I loved to sit outside with a blanket over my head on a windy day. Now I understand why I never missed a chance to do this. Living in the windiest city on the Peninsula was also a blessing. I still like to be in wind and notice the sounds it is when I get my best ideas and my biggest awareness.

Remember as discussed in Om twenty one, when you find yourself stressed notice how you are breathing. Most likely you will notice you are holding your breath or breathing from the chest or nasal. Taking in those deep belly breaths will give you physical relief, letting in the element of Air; helping to cleanse the blood, organs and muscles in your body releasing the tense energy and increasing your mental clarity. Keep up the deep breathing and you will find a sense of connection to the Spirit realm and enhanced psychic awareness.

_____

_____

_____

Air Element – Workbook twenty four

-<u>Monday</u>
How clear are your thoughts? Are they full of ether and unconditional love?
Write down the thoughts you had today that were, and those that were not?

_____   _____   _____

_____   _____   _____

~   What do you have more of?

_____   _____   _____

-<u>Tuesday</u>
Focus on the ones that were not of unconditional love. Why?

What can you do about changing the thoughts to be more loving?

_____   _____   _____

_____   _____   _____

<u>-Wednesday</u>
Are your thoughts clear? Do you know what it is you are here for?   Write or think about this.

_____

_____

<u>-Thursday</u>
Notice when thoughts are not clear and take a break and breathe in the element of air and ether to help.

How did this help?   _____

What did you notice?   _____

<u>-Friday</u>
Write or think about anything you noticed by being aware of your thoughts this week.

_____

_____

_____

_____

_____

~ ॐ ~

Water Element – How to Invoke the Cleansing

The Third Elemental force is Water; the element represents our emotions, motives, diet and exercise.

I myself have a bit of a fear of water in this lifetime and as I work to eliminate the fear from my life I do notice changes in my emotions and diet.

Water is the force of cleansing. Just hearing water rushing changes the way you feel. If you want to gain insight to seeing just below the surface of a situation you can use a cleansing ritual using the Water Element. A big step in growth is in letting old experiences flow away with the river, opening up space for new experiences to flow in.

Is your life like the rush of white water rapids or the calm peacefulness of a serene pool? Noticing the balance in movement in any river or stream and calling on this to aid in the balancing of your movement and emotions.

Although I have a fear of being in water I love to be near it. I have my favorite place near the San Lorenzo River where I do a lot of meditating and cleansing. This river is where I have found most of my 60 or so heart rocks. Before I approach the river I ask for the sign of collecting a heart rock if I am still on the right path. Most of the time I find one and sometimes I find lots.

Water can teach us the value of learning the lessons of our emotional experiences and the importance of communicating our knowledge to others. Opening your heart and letting the Water Element speak the true essence of who you are.

We are meant to speak our emotions, to feel them and then to release them when they no longer serve our purpose. This is how nature intended us to process but we are told, by employers, parents or others to hide them, to not feel or even show them.

When we follow this path we bury them inside never releasing them from our bodies. You cannot release what you do not feel or acknowledge.

Call on the Water Element to help in this process. Go to the ocean and focus on the water by breathing in and out with the tide. Take a bath and focus on seeing the water cleansing out the old emotions letting them go, or have a great cry over a good movie.

Notes:

_____

_____

_____

_____

Water Element – Workbook twenty five

-<u>Monday</u>
Find yourself a place where there is water; a stream, a river, a lake or the ocean.

Make this your spot to go when you need to release.

Write about the spot you found.

_____

_____

_____

_____

-Tuesday
Take time today to sit in your hot tub or make a nice hot bath. If you have neither, take a long hot shower. Use a sea salt scrub to cleanse your aura.

Thank the water for cleansing and blessing you.

-Wednesday
Today when you feel stress coming on, stop and find water, and wash your hands and face. Let the water run over your hands as you thank the water for cleansing and blessing you.

-Thursday
What have you noticed this week after letting water cleanse you? How has it helped?

_____ _____ _____

_____ _____ _____

-Friday
If you can have alone time tonight, watch a movie that makes you cry.

Have a good one (cry) -- release it all if you can.

How do you feel now?

_____

~ ॐ ~

Weekly Om – Twenty Six

Fire Element – How Fire Creates Change

As I am editing this passage California burns, having more than 1000 fires already this summer. Reading it now... I am reminded of the power and fear that fire creates, but also that it can be a necessary process for re growth.

Positive and beautiful things can come out of the destruction of fire. Out of the ashes, regrowth will be seen within time. Fire is the symbol of combustion and not a force to be taken lightly.

Fire is the element of heat and also of the Sacral and Solar Plexus Chakras. These centers being the core of our personal power, sexual energy and will. Your passion that burns with desire in these centers can create powerful positive energy. Focusing on this area in the body using fire to destroy old patterns then purify, transform and form more joyful creations. It is nature at its peak of growth, and warmth in human relationships. The power of Fire is transformation, changing its form, appearance and structure. This is done through its cleansing and purifying force.

As devastating as a forest fire is, it is Mother Nature's way of cleansing the land. The powers of transformation make fire a vital force to invoke for those in drastic need of changing their path. When using the Fire Element to create change, know that it will bring on a lesson or two along with that change. Utilizing the power of fire's destruction you can release what no longer serves you; from the ashes of fire a new form will appear.

By offering those things that are no longer needed to the flame you can release the energy behind it. One way of releasing and using the force of fire is to have a candle ritual.

Fire Element Candle Ritual
Carving in the candle a symbol to what no longer serves you and upon lighting the candle meditate on releasing this to the flame of fire until the symbols melt away, utilizing the power of fire to create the change that is needed.

147

_____

_____

_____

_____

Fire Element – Workbook twenty six

<u>-Monday</u>

Create a list of what you would like to release. Write down positive things that will appear in your life after releasing these items from your life.

_____   _____   _____

_____   _____   _____

_____   _____   _____

_____   _____   _____

<u>-Tuesday</u>

Gather up a bowl, fireplace or fire pit, a lighter, a piece of paper and pen. Take the first item on the above list and writing it on a piece of paper, write down everything about this item that is negative. Hold it in your hands and think about all of its negativity, feeling the effects in your body now. Then burn it – see and feel all the negativity leaving as you watch the flames burn into ashes.

~Wednesday
How do you feel after burning the item? Did anything positive happen? If you need to, do this again until it is gone.

_____ _____ _____

~Thursday
Move on to other items if you are ready, or continue to do the same one.

~Friday
Try the candle ritual -- keep lighting the candle each night until it will not light anymore.

Keep writing about changes you are seeing and feeling. Use this in the future to help you get rid of negative feelings, situations or relationships.

_____ _____ _____

_____ _____ _____

_____ _____ _____

_____ _____ _____

_____ _____ _____

_____ _____ _____

~ ॐ ~

Earth Element – How Does This Element Support Us?

I have been told by many healers and astrologers that I am all Earth. My rising and ascending signs are Earth; I love earth tone colors and gardening. I feel I need earth to keep me grounded. This is why it is so easy for me to manifest my thoughts into physical form and why I am so focused on doing so.

The Earth Element is the one of five elements representing a time of harvest, nourishment, and fertility. It is why I love the season of Autumn so much. This element is the center of balance and the place where energy becomes downward in movement, along the energy highway of manifestation. Through this gateway is where our dreams are manifested and born. It is the symbol of stability and being properly anchored or grounded.

The Earth Element is associated with the Root Chakra, with the bones, teeth and nails of the body. All of which are our support systems and foundations.

The energy frequencies flow from the Earth Element transforming the raw energy into matter, then forming all ideas and dreams into manifestation. Choose your focus then connect and channel this immense energy force. Apply its frequency with your own manifesting energy, creating your reality and making your dreams come true.

When these energetic centers are vibrating in harmony, you will be able to function effectively in the physical world maintaining all your own basic needs. Worrying about physical needs falls away, as you become aware of the abundance that the earth element has to offer.

A person that is not in harmony with these frequencies could be overly fearful of supporting themselves or very superficial in nature.

Look around and see the Earth gives us everything we need and the divine energy has put it all in place. There is abundance for us all! We just have to trust that and learn how to create it through the energy provided for us. Now is the time to focus on this energy to undertake the tasks that we are putting off as impossible. All you need is the will to call upon the Earth Element and your own Root Chakra to create and manifest your life!

Notes:

_____

_____

_____

_____

Earth Element – Workbook twenty seven

-Monday
Do something that puts you in nature today. Sit outside and enjoy a planet growing or a bird flying.

_____   _____   _____

-Tuesday
How did that make you feel? Can you fit more of nature into your life? List how you can do this.

_____   _____   _____

_____   _____   _____

_____   _____   _____

_____   _____   _____

-<u>Wednesday</u>
Start a garden, plant something in your garden or create a kitchen herb garden.

-<u>Thursday</u>
Sit on the ground close to the Earth, feel the vibrations that come from it.

Watch the sun set and listen for the sizzle of the sun hitting the ocean or horizon.

Feel that you are connected to it all, because you are!

-<u>Friday</u>
Sit outside in the night air looking at the stars and moon. I hope it is a full moon when you do this. If not, make it a point to do this the next one. See the wonder of the night sky as often as you can.

~ ॐ ~

Weekly Om – Twenty Eight

The Grounding Experience – How Do I Find My Center?

Grounding is a direct electrical connection to the earth. It works in the same way as an electronic circuit, or an indirect connection that operates as the result of electrical capacity between wireless equipment and the Earth.

When we are grounded we increase our sense of gravity giving us balance. We become centered, calm and receptive. We become confident, able to think and focus in a clear manner. This condition of receptivity and calmness occur when our brains produce more alpha rhythms.

When I am grounded I feel a sense of my whole body. I feel I am using all my muscles to hold myself upright, I am strong. I can think clearly and do not react to negativity in the same manner as when I am not grounded.

Parallel to our physical spine, there is a central column of subtle energy. This is the midline of the body, where the Chakras are located. The energy needs to run freely in order to maintain you as grounded and in good energetic health. When I hear others say I have no energy, I hear I am not grounded. If you want more energy then get yourself grounded first.

There are many inner pathways all working together and all eventually working within each other. For now let's just focus on the two pathways in midline. As an upright creature standing on our legs we move forward with our feet on the ground and our head in the air. These two major currents flow upward and downward. The upward current is called _liberation,_ as it begins from the earth in an upward movement it rises us up toward awareness, gaining increasing freedom from limitations of the physical world. When we have blocks in this flow we begin to have compulsive behaviors and you might be limiting yourself from freedom by constricting or destructive patterns. The downward current begins with consciousness and descends toward the earth; this is the current of _manifestation._ Beginning at the crown as an idea and sending the energy to the physical plane manifesting into a finished product. If your downward flow is blocked you may have lots of ideas and talk about your dreams but you may never see them to completion.

It is essential to have both currents flowing freely to be a balanced individual. You need to liberate yourself from fixed or limiting forms in order to experience the true nature of expanded consciousness, and in order to live your dreams you need to be able to manifest them into visions, then into reality, in order to influence the world around you.

Clearing the Pathways Meditation
Lay on your back, with a pillow or bolster under your knees for lower back support. Focus on your breathing slowing it down and smoothing it out. Feel the Belly rising when you inhale and falling when you exhale. Send the breath downward from the Crown Chakra (crown of the head) to the Root Chakra (tail bone) for five breaths, then reverse from the Root Chakra to the Crown Chakra for the count of five breaths.

Then focusing on the Root, visualize a root - sending it from the tailbone down into the floor, down in to the foundation, then down into the dirt....deep down in to the earth's core.... Sending you strength and energy. Roll yourself back up and move to standing. Spread out the toes and press the ball of the foot firmly into the ground feeling more centered and grounded to the earth.

Notes:

_____

_____

_____

The Grounding Experience – Workbook twenty eight

-Monday
Go to the beach or take a salt bath. Ask the water to cleanse and bless you. Do a grounding meditation. How did this make you feel?

_____   _____   _____

-<u>Tuesday</u>
Stand with your feet firmly against the ground. Feel the whole foot, left and
right touching the Earth. Repeat until you understand what being connected
to it feels like. How long did this take? Is it getting easier to understand?

_____   _____   _____

_____   _____   _____

-<u>Wednesday</u>
When you feel stress today, take in a deep breath and visualize a root from
your tailbone down into the feet and into the Earth. Take three more deep
breaths before responding or reacting to the stress. Did you notice any
change?

_____   _____   _____

-<u>Thursday</u>
Before you start your day today stand tall, stretch your arms over head. Then
pick up the heels of the feet and lightly tap them on the ground, almost like
bouncing on your heels. Take in deep breaths as you do this. Keep it up until
you feel like you are grounded and ready for your day.

-<u>Friday</u>
Do this week's meditation for fifteen minutes, as you meditate take the left
foot in your hands and rub your foot, find tension spots and press on them for
a few seconds, repeat on the right foot.

~ ॐ ~

Chakras – What Are They?

My favorite things in the world are my Chakras, unseen to the naked eye but everything to me. Energy is everything and everything is energy. When you learn how to create it, use it and how to fix it when you need to... you feel free of limitations.

The Chakras run up the spine within your aura, there is a lot of information associated with them and about them. I will mostly focus on the seven that align the spine, the major centers of this system.

When we can keep our Chakras at a balanced level, we have balanced energy. Our well-being will be healthy, meaning good physical and mental health. Being able to live in the present moment and being grounded, living life to your fullest. This feeling will then create more energy and you will feel like you can take on more and do many things with ease.

Our journey through life is a challenging one. The journey that occurs at the Chakra level happens in this fashion. Energy comes into the body through the Chakras, distributing these levels of energy through each center and then each center sends to the body part that it governs over, giving them the energy to run your body, mind and spirit.

When life becomes challenging, as it does for all of us at times, we find ways to cope.

In our energy centers there are two ways of coping with our difficulties. We can increase our energy in those centers to help us deal with it. Or we are decreasing our energy, being in denial of it or running away. This being the basic flight or fight response programmed into our survival instincts.

Examples of increasing your energy would include creating a fever to fight bacteria, gathering information to gain wisdom about a situation, staying with a project until its completion and taking in deep breaths before approaching an issue.

Decreasing your energy is a way of trying to get away from a threat, dissociating to minimize pain or fear, avoiding people, not caring, running.

As you engage these defenses they become hard wired into your Chakra system. They unconsciously become habitual patterns, regardless of whether or not these patterns really work for you. When repeating patterns over and over again, you create either excessive or deficient Chakras. If you have patterns of increasing your energy too much you might find yourself overcompensating or fixating on things, or creating excessive behaviors. Habitual patterns of deficiency are those of avoidance or running from life.

What are your habitual patterns? Do you find yourself in flight or fight too often? If you are, then you must be seeing signs in your body and your life that are telling you to slow down and get some peace. Do you run from others, life or avoid hard topics of conversation? If so, then you might find that nothing gets accomplished.

Balancing out the Chakras daily and noticing what your patterns are, you can start to make fast and easy changes to your life.

Chakra Explanation and Meditation
All journeys begin with a single step. You can only take that step by making solid contact with the Earth, the element of the first Chakra.

- ~ <u>Root Chakra</u> (base of the tail bone). This links the individual to the physical world; grounds us to the Earth and acts as a support system. The associated body parts are bones, teeth, nails.
  - Breathing in through the petals and out through the stem focusing on the color of red
  - Excessive Characteristics (EC) - slow movements, overeating, material fixation, excessive spending
  - Deficient Characteristics (DC) – fear, anxiety, anorexia restlessness difficulty manifesting
  - Balanced characteristics (BC) – Being rounded, good physical health sense of safety; the ability to be still, present, and in the moment.

The second Chakra is the element of Water as. Our bodies are made up mostly of water, and within these bodies flow our emotions, desires, our wants and needs, our feelings and sensations.

- ~ <u>Sacral Chakra</u> (in the sacrum) associated body parts are the low back, the bladder, and the reproductive system.
  - Breathing into the stem and out through the petals focusing on the color of orange
  - EC- sexual addictions, excessive mood swings, poor boundaries, emotional dependency
  - DC- emotional numbness, fear of change, lack of desire or passion, excess boundaries, boredom
  - BC- graceful movements, ability to embrace change, emotional intelligence, healthy boundaries, passion.

From Earth to Water to Fire

~ <u>Solar Plexus Chakra</u> (above the navel) energy center for your power and your will. Impulses such as desire and wishes blend here. Associated body parts are stomach, liver, gall bladder and nervous system.
- Breathing into the petals and out through the stem focusing on yellow
- EC- dominating, controlling, arrogant, stubborn attracted to sedatives
- DC – lack of energy, poor digestion, tendency to be cold, low self esteem
- BC- responsible, good self discipline, warm, able to take risks

~ <u>Heart Chakra</u> (center of the chest) is the very center of the Chakra system as well as the heart of our being and the chamber from which we give and receive love. Associated body parts are the heart, upper back, rib cage, chest, lower lungs, and the circulatory system.
- Breathing the petals open and exhaling them closed focusing on color Green
- EC- codependency, poor boundaries, jealously, being a martyr or pleaser
- DC- withdrawn, lonely, lack of empathy, fear of intimacy
- BC- caring, compassionate, accepting, peaceful, centered

~ <u>Throat Chakra</u> (base of the throat). This Chakra is about opening your voice, speaking your truth and freeing your creativity. Through communication you connect, expand and unite with others creating your world as you go. Associated body parts are lungs, vocal cords, bronchial passages, throat, thyroid, jaw and neck
- Breathing into the petals and exhaling out through the stem focusing on the light blue
- EC- talking too much, gossiping, excessive loudness, inability to keep confidences
- DC- difficulty putting things into words, fear of speaking, shyness, weak voice
- BC- full voice, clear communication, good listener, good sense of timing and rhythm, lives life creatively

~ <u>Third Eye Chakra</u> (mid forehead) is the center of intuition and inner vision. Associated body parts are, the pineal gland, face, eyes, nose, sinus, and pituitary gland
- Breathe into the stem and out the petals seeing the color indigo or dark blue
- EC- hallucinations, obsessions, nightmares, difficulty concentrating
- DC- lack of imagination, difficulty visualizing, denial
- BC- strong intuition, insight, good memory and dream recall - has a vision for life

Last but not least .... In the true meaning of the word "yoga" as union we have the

~ **Crown Chakra** (top of the head) your individual point of awareness which connects us with the Divine Intelligence, the universe, knowing there is no separation. This is your higher power, your spirit and your knowledge of understanding that we are a spiritual being in a physical body. Associated body parts are brain, cerebellum and skull.
- Breathing into the petals and out of the stem focusing on the color purple
- EC – dissociation from the body, spiritual addiction, confusion, living in your head, disconnect from spirit.
- DC –closed mindedness, learning difficulties, rigid belief systems, apathy and spiritual cynicism
- BC – spiritual connection, wisdom and mastery, intelligence, open mindedness, ability to assimilate and analyze information.

It is the tremendous experience of becoming conscious,
which nature has laid upon mankind, which entitles
the most diverse cultures in a common task.
--C. G. Jung

Notes:

_____

_____

_____

Chakras - Workbook twenty nine

<u>-Monday</u>
Put in your schedule today to take fifteen minutes and do the Chakra meditation above, reading it and touching the area where the Chakras are located. Then close your eyes and focus on each one, visualizing your lotus flower opening and closing. What did you notice?

_____   _____   _____

_____   _____   _____

<u>-Tuesday</u>
Before you get out of bed do the meditation from memory. Don't worry if you have forgotten anything. Just do what you can and what you remember.

Did you notice anything telling you which Chakras are out of balance? Keep listening all day today.

_____   _____   _____

_____   _____   _____

<u>-Wednesday</u>

If you have any ideas about which Chakras might be out of balance. Do the lotus flower meditation with one of those Chakras.

-<u>Thursday</u>
Look back in the other workbooks that you have completed and see if you can tell which Chakras are out of balance by other things you have listed.

_____   _____   _____

_____   _____   _____

-<u>Friday</u>
Take thirty minutes today to do the Chakra meditation in full and to stay on each Chakra for a good four to five minutes.

Do you notice anything?

_____   _____   _____

_____   _____   _____

_____   _____   _____

~ ॐ ~

Root Chakra – What is Being Grounded?

You should have an idea of what being grounded feels like and is. If not, then I suggest you should focus more on doing grounding meditations and focus on the Root Chakra. In your free time do things that help ground you like gardening, going to the beach and being with nature.

The first Chakra is the Root Chakra located at the base of the spine at the tail bone. We have already learned its color, element and associated body parts in Om twenty nine. Use it as a guide for this and the next six Oms.

The name root means support or foundation and is what grounds us to the Earth plane. The human challenges and gift; is to feel safe and secure in the physical plane and to manifest to meet our basic needs. Our Soul's desire is to feel nurtured and nourished. That is the experience of being whole and belonging to the whole.

It is an act of power to be able to recognize that you are grounded and to feel the present moment, feeling your feet firmly connected to the Earth as you stand tall; with your mind not wandering into the past or in the future. You are not giving away your energy to anything other than enjoying and living in this moment.

The power is yours! Use it or lose it!
--Melissa Stone

Slow yourself down and start to make all the little things matter. Every smile you make and every step you take is all important in your life. I hear from so many that they have no time for themselves or to slow down. Are you not worth it? Taking time to just "Be" with yourself is so important in your relationship with yourself. You are worth that extra moment to spend with yourself to take that deep breath and bring yourself fully into focus. When you are fully grounded you make less mistakes, you will make better choices, and you will notice less drama in your life. There will be more time for all those projects you think you will never complete.

Root Chakra Meditation

You can find ten to fifteen minutes in your day and just sit and listen to your breathing. You know now how to see where you are breathing from and how to slow it down. Changing the breathing pattern to the belly, slow it down and smooth it out. Notice where you are holding your stress and send the breath there relaxing it and the whole body. When the mind starts to wander and you notice it doing so, send the thoughts away and go back to your breathing. Then focus on the Root Chakra at the base of the tailbone. Imagine it is a lotus flower. Inhale the petals open and exhale the petals closed giving it the color of Red. Sit with this for a moment.

Notes:

_____

_____

_____

Root Chakra – Workbook thirty

-Monday
Before you get out of bed do the Root Chakra meditation, then get out of bed slowly taking deep breaths, raise your arms up stretching over head then move to a downward facing dog yoga pose. Your body is in a V shape, hands shoulder width apart fanning out the fingers and feet hips distance apart. Send the heels toward the floor and the breast bone towards the knees, inhaling in and sending the breath to the tail bone (Root Chakra). Visualize the energy going down the legs, grounding you to the Earth.

Walk the legs in place and get a good stretch.

-Tuesday
What did you notice different about your day yesterday by grounding
yourself before you started your day? Make a list, were you more organized,
did things seem to go smoothly or did you feel good? If nothing do it again
and start to notice what is happening and how you feel.

_____   _____   _____

_____   _____   _____

-Wednesday
Do the Meditation above before you start your day and when you start to feel
stressed, do it throughout the day. Sit and just imagine a root coming from
the Root Chakra, sending it into the ground. What did you notice today?

_____   _____   _____

_____   _____   _____

-Thursday
Get outside today. Feel the Earth, plant something or hold some rocks. Thank
the Earth for Blessing you and grounding you today.

-Friday
Treat yourself to a hot salt bath or go to the beach, river or some form of
water. Thank the water for Blessing you and grounding you.

~ ॐ ~

Weekly Om – Thirty One

Sacral Chakra – What Are You Doing with Your Emotions?

Moving up the body along the spine you will find the second Chakra, located directly below the navel (belly button), the Sacral Chakra. This Chakra is the element of water, with our bodies being made mostly of water, within these bodies flow our emotions, desires, our wants, our needs, and our sensations. Pleasure is the motivating principal of this Chakra, along with governing our emotions.

Once the foundation is set and the survival needs are satisfied in the Root, we can then turn to the Sacral (Chakra) to find pleasure, promoting things such as play, laughter and experiencing beauty, leading to being content and at peace.

Being in denial of simple pleasures in life can lead to overindulgence and addiction. Emotion and pleasure are made of feelings and sensations. They give us a powerful source of information about our well-being. Understanding the complex nature of your emotions is necessary in order to stay afloat in the water element of this second Chakra.

When your right to feel is challenged guilt arises. Remember guilt tells us we should not feel or want or need. Guilt can be a valid emotion if it is caused by us hurting someone, including ourselves, by our overindulgence or addiction. Knowing when guilt is blocking your feelings or when it is valid is how to unlock the balance in this Chakra.

Thinking about how your emotions have been lately; are they balanced? Have you been feeling your emotions? Do you let emotions flow when they come up? Do they come up at the wrong times? Do old emotions come up when you are in new situations and you put these old emotions on to people that have nothing to do with them?

These are questions that need to be answered in order to help you balance out this energy center and your emotions.

To ensure you are keeping it in balance make sure you are not all work and no play. Pleasure is a wonderful important part of been human. Make sure that you are seeing the beauty that is all around and indulging in the pleasure of life. Feeling like a kid again helps to bring, balance and is a lot of fun at the same time.

Sacral Chakra Connection Meditation

Make a connection to the second Chakra by sitting in a comfortable place placing the hands below the navel, focus on breathing into the Sacrum. Visualize it as a lotus flower, inhale the petals open and exhale the petals closed, giving it the color of orange. Feel your emotions balancing out and connecting with pleasure in your life.

Notes:

_____

_____

_____

_____

Sacral Chakra – Workbook thirty one

-Monday

Looking at your emotional state of being, how would you say you are most of the time?

Excessive (overly emotional), deficient (afraid to show emotions) or balanced (feel and express your emotions). Do the Connection meditation and focus on balancing out your emotions.

_____   _____   _____

-Tuesday
Make a list of things you like to do. Now look at the ones that you have not done in a while and put some in your schedule for this week.

_____   _____   _____

_____   _____   _____

-Wednesday
When driving to work today notice all things that please the eye. A flower on the side of the freeway, a nice car (not desirous - just notice its beauty) or someone's wonderful smile.

-Thursday
Do something you have not done in a long time, act like a kid. Swing at the park, play ball or run for no reason.

-Friday
Take yourself out to eat to a place that has all your favorites, get dressed up and wear an outfit you have been saving for a special occasion. Cook yourself an awesome healthy dinner and use 'the good china.'

~ ॐ ~

Solar Plexus – How Are You Creating Your Power?

Traveling up the spine to the center of the body is the power Chakra. As we ground ourselves in the Root, balance out our emotions and pleasure in the Sacrum, the energy then rises to the third Chakra. It has the potential to become your personal power, but only if your will-power will allow it to become the personal power that is. This power is what will run your body and become more will power.

You need this power to get you through the difficult parts of your journey. Just as solar panels take the sun's energy converting it into power which can then run your household or other equipment. Your Solar Plexus has the means to run enough power to your body to get you through your day or life's challenges. You can get through anything that life puts in front of you if you focus on this as your power center. Mastering this energy will get you through anything.

Are you giving away your energy too often? Do you find yourself being in situations where you are not keeping your power? Not speaking your mind or letting stress get to you. These are all times when you give away your power.

The power of the third Chakra depends on the strength of your will. This quality will change your situation into the desired outcome through your intentions. To blend the intention with the will, begin by making the intention in your consciousness then let it flow through the Chakra system generating the body's metabolism, making energy. If the intention and the energy are out of balance or are not in sync the will is weakened – you either have lots of energy and are without clear direction, or have good intentions with not enough energy to fulfill them. When in balance the will is strong and your personal power naturally arises.

Success is not the result of spontaneous combustion. You must set yourself on fire.
--Reggie Leach

175

Paying attention to what increases your energy and what situations suppress it will provide a clear purpose to your focus. Over time this will train your impulse into mastery serving you for the rest of your life!

Notes:

_____

_____

_____

_____

Solar Plexus – Workbook thirty two

-Monday
How do you feel when you use your power? Do you give it away or misuse it? Make a list of how you could change these things by stating your truth or using your energy for good.

_____   _____   _____

_____   _____   _____

-Tuesday
Do some stomach exercises today. On your back knees bent, hands clasped behind your head or across your chest if you tend to pull your neck. On the exhale do 20 to 25 crunches. Focus on the Solar Plexus glowing bright yellow as you do these crunches, feel its power.

-Wednesday
When you get out of the shower today stand in front of the mirror, look at your belly and try to roll it. Awaken the Solar Plexus by doing my favorite belly dance move - belly rolls. Take a deep breath in as you pull in the bottom of the belly, roll it up to the top and exhale as you roll it back down. Move slowly at first then try to speed it up and change direction. Have fun with your belly rolls.

-Thursday
Practice will power today and give up something. When you are craving or thinking about it go to your Solar Plexus and focus on this fire ball giving you the power to say no.   Maybe even stand up for yourself today.

-Friday
Is there something you have wanted to say or do, that you feel is too big a risk? Do it today or at least take the next step. Free your personal power.

~ ॐ ~

Weekly Om – Thirty Three

Heart Chakra – Is Love the Essence of Life?

Love is the ultimate healer, providing assurance of survival. The desire to receive love is a basic need for humans, but the art of giving of love in an unconditional manner transcends the ego. It overflows from the Heart Chakra and fulfills the spirit.

The heart's task is to find balance in giving and receiving unconditional love. To live with an open heart, to treat others as well as things, with honor and respect no matter who or what they are. This love will naturally arise when you find the divine power of the Heart Chakra.

The result of this power is the ability to love unconditionally. The element of the heart is air, ruled by the breath and your thoughts. Breathing can be a way to cleanse away any blocks from your heart center. Becoming aware of your thought patterns can help you to see where you are closing your heart. Keeping walls up because you have been hurt in the past only closes down your heart from receiving and giving unconditional love.

We need to feel the hurt to experience and realize what unconditional love is. If there was no pain to feel in this world we would not understand or appreciate things of pleasure. Learning to move through pain, to let go of the past, and to live in the present moment is just the beginning of being in balance. When life is hard, turn inward and love yourself. Find the support of friends, family, yoga, meditation, and take care of yourself to regain the control of your heart. Keeping it open and full of unconditional love for all is joy.

I like to give myself love by taking a hot bath in some sea salts, give myself a facial, eat a good meal or get a massage. When you don't feel like doing it is when you really need to. As a massage therapist I hear lots of excuses for canceling an appointment, but the most bizarre is that the client is too stressed to get their massage. This my friends is when you need to get unconditional love most.

It is only with the heart that one can see rightly; what is essential is invisible to the eye.
--Antoine de Saint-Exupery

179

There have been many times that I have been on my therapist's massage table releasing my stress. Two days before I was to film my workout DVD, my computer crashed. All of my writings including the beginning of this book, all my financial information and my script for the DVD gone? I had set up a whole day of pampering beginning with a massage for the day before I filmed. I wanted to cancel, but my spirit won that day and I went. I got the help and support I needed to keep me in balance, keep me loving myself so I could get through this tough time. Find a support system for those days when you need a little help in loving yourself.

Notes:

_____

_____

_____

_____

Heart Chakra – Workbook thirty three

-Monday
How compassionate are you? Make a list of ways you could be more empathetic towards others. List out those people that you need to work on loving more and how you could show more love to them.

_____   _____   _____

_____   _____   _____

-Tuesday

Before you get up today place your hands on your heart and breathe into them. Focus on the heart being open and full of green energy. Do this until you feel open and loving, then get up and start your day.

-Wednesday

Forgive someone today. Make a list of grudges you are holding on to and decide which ones you can let go of and do so. Do the releasing techniques, meditations in this book or tell the person your forgive them and love them.

_____   _____   _____

_____   _____   _____

-Thursday

Make it a point today to do random acts of kindness to one person that really needs it, or to many. What did you do? How did that make you feel?

_____   _____   _____

-Friday

Make a gratitude list, of people, places and things. Express your appreciation to everyone around you today.

_____   _____   _____

_____   _____   _____

~ ॐ ~

Throat Chakra – How Vibration Heals the Voice

Moving up to the top of the spine is the Chakra of creativity, the Throat Chakra, where all talent and communication begin. Placing your fingers on the throat and taking in a deep breath feeling the vibrations of this essential fifth Chakra, as you move the air in and out of the lungs. The vibration is where the communication lays and awaits for its creation to begin. To commune, the root word of communication means "to be one with."

Located with the vocal cords and the pituitary gland, the Throat Chakra is the energy center for all your communication and your creativity. The energy will flow up the spine and act as a filter for the body's raw energy, giving it a voice as it passes through the fifth Chakra. Then it will continue up to the consciousness level to the Crown Chakra - but we will get to that later - adding in any creative thoughts as it flows through and up. Ever feel like the ideas are flowing?

The rhythmic vibration speaks your truth that comes from your spirit. The ego is what stops it in the throat, preventing it from coming out, if and when you are not speaking your truth. When we do this we know; it throws the throat Chakra out of balance, and we lose our personal power.

Using your core and the will from the Solar Plexus you will find it now easy to speak and live your core's truth, authentically bringing you back to the connection with your Spirit!

I have been working for the last four years at a local drug rehabilitation center part time. I teach a yoga class with meditation and I give energy healing and massage to those in need. This work has opened my eyes to a lot of things. I am a being that likes life in balance and I always have been. Addiction has touched my life through the partners I choose and with my father. Although I never lived with him or knew him, his addiction touched me only on a spiritual level. Addiction is a misuse of your creativity. I feel those that are battling addiction are very talented

To live a creative life, we must lose our fear to be wrong.
--Joseph Chilton Pearce

and creative beings. When they are not clear in the Throat Chakra or how to direct this creative energy, it then becomes directed in a negative way towards the Sacral Chakra as overindulgence in pleasure.

If you are battling addiction get some help in detoxifying (detoxing) your body. It is best to find a place that does this without medications - if your doctor agrees, find some counseling and find your creative outlet to discover balance and positive pleasure.

Notes:

_____

_____

_____

_____

Throat Chakra – Workbook thirty four

-Monday
Do you have any creative outlets? How often do you partake in them?

_____   _____   _____

_____   _____   _____

How can you do more creative things?

_____   _____   _____

_____   _____   _____

-Tuesday
Is there someone with whom you have miscommunications? Sit quietly and focus on the Throat Chakra, visualizing sending the light blue energy of this Chakra to this person and see the miscommunication clearing. Did you notice any change?

_____   _____   _____

-Wednesday
Do some neck stretches, drop the right ear towards the right shoulder, feel the stretch in the left side of the neck. See the Chakra as a light blue flower opening up, repeat on other side. Do this throughout the day.

-Thursday
Sing in the shower, car or anywhere today, expressing your voice. At the end of the day sit and meditate while chanting the word OM, notice and feel the vibration as you do.

-Friday
Dance today, freeing your creativity as you dance. You can go out dancing or dance in your living room.

~ ॐ ~

The Third Eye – What Does it Mean to Really See?

As the Throat Chakra purifies the sound, the Third Eye filters through the visions, thus being the center of illumination. It is your door to seeing visions and having the wisdom of intuition. When you are living with a balanced Third Eye you will see everything unfolding as you live. This gives great confidence to your decision making and your dreams.

This Chakra has the capability of seeing beyond this physical world, seeing the energy of other realms. By training your consciousness to be focused it will open this passageway between your two physical eyes. To see visions from this center is an immense gift, not to be taken lightly, one that can be attained by anyone with practice, patience and your focused attention. You can start with just five minutes a day. Eventually you will want to focus more time to this skill and somehow that time will just appear for you.

It is through this insight we start to perceive our patterns, seeing the meaning behind them and then creating the energy to free ourselves from repeating them, moving us to the top of the liberation highway at the Crown Chakra of understanding and wisdom.

When you visualize positive images you want to manifest, you are likely to create that positive outcome. The universe knows no right from wrong and will create at your command. Focusing on negative images will send the Third Eye spinning into manifesting the negativity for you. You will draw upon that energy behind the images and will create what you wish for.

Remember the old saying,
'Be careful what you wish for'
-- Author unknown

Connection to The Third Eye: Meditation

Moving to Childs Pose, sitting on your knees place the two big toes together, knees slightly apart and the forehead against the floor. Connecting the Third Eye to the Earth. Grounding yourself through this Chakra, visualize the Chakra as open. Inhale in through the Solar Plexus feeling the raw energy flow upward along the spine. Feel it now moving through the Throat Chakra and up into the Third Eye. Exhale out from the Third Eye flowing upward through the Crown Chakra.

Repeat for three breaths.

Reverse for three more breaths, inhaling into the Crown Chakra and downward into the Third Eye back to the Solar Plexus Chakra.

Write down any visions you might have during this meditation.

_____

_____

_____

Notes:

_____

_____

_____

Third Eye – Workbook thirty five

-Monday
Make an effort to Connect with your Third Eye today. Breathe into it for a bit when you wake in the morning. Stop before you make decisions today and ask your intuition for guidance, take in deep breaths, be still and try to hear what your intuition is trying to tell you. Even if you hear something you do not like, listen!

-Tuesday
Play the phone game, when the phone rings before looking at the caller ID try to guess who it is. How many times were you correct? Keep playing this.

_____   _____   _____

_____   _____   _____

-Wednesday
Play my color match game, get fourteen 5 x 7 cards and write these colors on two of each of the cards - red, orange, yellow, green, light blue, dark blue and purple. Then turn them over and spread them out make sure they are mixed up. Turn one card over and then one more. If they match set them aside. If they don't match turn them back over and see if you can make all matches. Start to time yourself and see if you can get faster and faster.

-Thursday
Before making any decisions today try to look at it from your Third Eye. Ask yourself for guidance instead of from others today.

-<u>Friday</u>
Get a blank piece of paper and color pens.

Do the meditation and without thinking about anything or what to draw start drawing.

Sit quietly drawing for as long as you want, then put it away and look at it tomorrow, seeing what you can in your intuition drawing. Put it away and mark your calendar to look at your intuition picture again in about a month. Did the vision come to reality or does it tell you anything?

~ ॐ ~

Weekly Om – Thirty Six

Crown Chakra - How to Gain Wisdom

The Crown Chakra, like the brain, is the center of your consciousness and the operating system of the body and Chakras. What I like to call my higher power, the engineer of the body. This is known as the individual point of awareness connecting you with the Divine Intelligence.

When you are aware of this unity and know there is no separation from you and the Divine, you can go beyond awareness to a more enlightened state of being. Yogis spend their lives practicing this in order to achieve the ultimate freedom, but only few will achieve full enlightenment. Most of us will have moments of enlightenment giving us that taste of liberation. From these moments of awaking we gain divine wisdom, using this wisdom to create and manifest your reality.

Look around you and see what the divine consciousness looks like. What have you manifested in your life? If your conscious thoughts are not what you see on the physical plane then you have more work to do within the other Chakras.

Working in the rehabilitation setting I hear a lot about the higher power. The twelve steps basically say to turn it all over to this power. This is what we all should be doing; balancing out the energy in the Chakras, clearing them and our Karma, then letting the Crown run the show. When you are in need and feeling like you are in a struggle, focus on the Crown Chakra and allow it to balance it all out. Feel like this is your spirit guiding you in the right direction. This does take trust, which we will get into later.

Keep the faith and trust that the spirit, YOUR SPIRIT, will guide you in the right direction.

Clearing and Protecting the Chakras: Meditation
During a relaxing session focus on bringing in white light and energy into the Crown Chakra, sending the breath down through all the Chakras and exhaling out what no longer serves you through the Root Chakra. Then cover yourself in this bubble of white light.

_____

_____

_____

_____

Crown Chakra – Workbook thirty six

-<u>Monday</u>
Find a great spot during the day, like under an awesome tree, and lay down on the ground and watch the sky for a bit. Feel the seventh Chakra above the crown of the head and breathe into it as you focus on the sky, clouds or birds flying around. Notice it all.

-<u>Tuesday</u>
Do Monday's exercise at night. Watch the stars to find shooting stars, or pay attention to the moon. Connect with the night sky.

-<u>Wednesday</u>
Create a quite place in your home and place symbols of things that are peaceful to you in this space. When in this space feel comfort and a connection to your spirit.

<u>-Thursday</u>
Get a book that speaks of Spirituality, like any of those listed in the back of this book, and start reading it at least fifteen minutes a day.

<u>-Friday</u>
Sitting quietly tonight let your thoughts race, but instead of being in your head thinking them, sit back and watch the movie of your thoughts. Let them roll without judgment or taking any action. See where these thoughts lead you. Write down these thoughts. Did any ideas come up, or maybe you remembered things you were forgetting?

_____

_____

_____

~ ॐ ~

Weekly Om – Thirty Seven

Attachment – When the Chakras are Excessive

Attachment is when the Chakras have too much energy flowing through them. The word attachment means: a connection by which one thing is connected to another. When this attachment becomes excessive it can mean your Chakras have become excessive, leading to compulsive behaviors and/or physical imbalances. Each Chakra has its own influence on certain aspects of your life as well as having their own colors and ties to the elements. Although we went over in the Om twenty nine, I will again list out the excessive behaviors related to each Chakra.

~ *Root Chakra*, (color of red and Earth Element) when excessive can stimulate behaviors of overeating, material fixation, greed, excessive spending or overworking.

~ *Sacral Chakra*, (color of orange and Water Element) when excessive can create behaviors of addiction, mood swings, poor boundaries, sexual addictions, and emotional dependency.

~ *Solar Plexus Chakra*, (color of yellow and Fire Element) when excessive you may have controlling behaviors, be dominating, have addictions to sedatives, be hyperactive or compulsively focused toward goals.

~ *Heart Chakra*, (color of green and Air Element) when this Chakra is excessive you may be codependent, display martyr behaviors, or spend too much time trying to please others.

~ *Throat Chakra*, (color of light blue and Ether/Sound Element) when excessive in the throat you may find yourself gossiping, talking too much or having difficulty being silent.

~ *Third Eye Chakra* (color of dark blue and Light Element) when excessive you might be experiencing nightmares, have difficulty in concentrating, have obsessions or fantasize excessive.

~ *Crown Chakra* (color purple and the Element of Spirit/Thought) When the Crown is excessive you may experience a disconnection from spirit, excessive attachments or living in your head (thinking too much).

197

When we can notice what our behaviors are we can then see where the changes are needed within our energy centers or Chakras. We learn to notice in order to start the process to becoming more balanced within our energy centers.

Notes:

_____

_____

_____

_____

Attachment – Workbook thirty seven

-Monday
Looking at the above list pick one of the Chakras that you feel might be excessive.

_____

See this Chakra as a lotus flower, see its color and start spinning the vision as you breathe. See the results of your excessiveness as you spin your vision, like addiction or gossiping, leaving as you see the Chakra spinning.

How do you feel after this exercise?

_____

-<u>Tuesday</u>
Using the same Chakra pick one of the exercises you liked from that Chakra's
workbook. Perform that exercise.

-<u>Wednesday</u>
Have you noticed any behaviors or energy changing? Start over on Monday's
exercise using a different Chakra this time.

_____   _____   _____

_____   _____   _____

-<u>Thursday</u>
Using that same Chakra as Wednesday, pick one of the exercises you liked
from that Chakra's workbook. Perform that exercise.

-<u>Friday</u>
Have seven blank pieces of paper near you and color pens, do the Chakra
meditation after focusing on each one, draw and color each one its correct
color and see what comes up for you.

~ ॐ ~

Weekly Om – Thirty Eight

Abandonment - When Chakras are Deficient

Abandonment is when there is not enough energy running through the Chakra system. The word abandonment means; to surrender your power or to give up. When you notice yourself giving in to abandonment behaviors it might just be that your Chakras are deficient. When you are not receiving in energy you may become depleted and that is when the imbalances begin. Physical pain can act as the clues for you to see where the balancing needs to take place. Again study this list to see where you need balancing out.

~ **Root Chakra** (associated body parts are the bones, teeth and nails) If deficient in the root you might have fear, anxiety, resistance to structure or difficulty in manifesting.

~ **Sacral Chakra** (low back, bladder and reproductive system) when this Chakra is deficient you might show signs of emotional numbness, a fear of change, boredom or avoidance of pleasure.

~ **Solar Plexus** (stomach, liver, gall bladder and Nervous System) this power Chakra when deficient will have signs of poor digestion, low self-esteem, weakness in will power and lack of energy.

~ **Heart Chakra** (heart, upper back, rib cage and circulatory system) feeling of loneness, lack of empathy, fear of intimacy may appear when this Chakra is deficient.

~ **Throat Chakra** (lungs, vocal cords, bronchial passages, throat, thyroid, jaw and neck) when deficient in this energy center you might have difficulty putting things into words, fear of speaking or excessive shyness.

~ **Third Eye Chakra** (eyes, nose, sinus and pituitary gland) Deficient characteristics may be lack of imagination, denial insensitivity or difficulty in visualizing or meditating.

~ **Crown Chakra** (brain and skull) Being deficient in the crown may cause spiritual cynicism, a closed mind, learning difficulties or a rigid belief system.

Along with behaviors, physical symptoms can give you clues to tell you which Chakra is out of balance. When we pay attention to what our bodies are telling us we can change how our energy flows, giving us peace of mind, body and spirit.

_____

_____

_____

_____

Abandonment - Workbook thirty eight

-Monday
Looking at the above list, which of the Chakras do you feel might be deficient?

_____   _____   _____

See this Chakra as a lotus flower, see its color and start spinning the vision as you breathe. See the results of your deficiency, like fear of intimacy or having shyness.

How do you feel after this exercise?

_____

-Tuesday
Using the same Chakra, pick one of the exercises you liked from that Chakra's workbook. Perform that exercise.

_____

-Wednesday
Have you noticed any behaviors or energy changing? Start over on Monday's exercise using a new Chakra now.

_____ _____ _____

-Thursday
Using that same Chakra pick one of the exercises you liked from that Chakra's workbook. Perform that exercise.

-Friday
Have seven blank pieces of paper and colored pens or pencils near you. Do the Chakra meditation. After focusing on each one, draw and color each one with its correct color and see what comes up for you.

~ ॐ ~

Chi – What Is It?

The subtle energy that runs through and around the body is called Chi (chee) in Chinese Medicine. Many cultures call this Chi by other names; in Western Medicine it is called biofields. This energy or Chi runs through the Chakras and the organs in the body giving you your life, thus being our "life force energy". It is not seen, just like the air we breathe, but it is there.

You can attune yourself to feel it and sometimes hear it. People that are attuned to feeling Chi can heal and telepathically communicate. If you have ever answered someone's question before they ask it, that is you being attuned to their chi.

Feeling Chi exercise:
Rub your hands together vigorously until they become hot, and then slowly start to pull them apart. Feel the tingling in your hands? The heat of the energy you just created is chi.

This is what I feel when balancing out someone's energy. The energy or Chi can feel chaotic, strong, fussy, like an electric shock; or there can be lack of energy. When the Chi is not balanced in your body it can cause stress, pain, discomfort and illness.

Clearing and Calming Chi Meditation
Sit quietly try to feel the energy (chi) running through your body, focusing on calming it and letting it flow. If you have pain or tension anywhere, visualize the chi flowing into it and through it.

Notes:

_____

_____

_____

_____

Chi – Workbook thirty nine

-Monday
Sitting quietly focus on the air around you. See it as white light swirling about as you breathe in and out. Do this throughout the day. Feel the energy coming in your body from this Chi.

-Tuesday
Stand with feet hip distance apart slight bend at the knees. Bring the right hand up to the right shoulder, palm facing out and bring the left hand up to the left shoulder extending the arm out palm facing in. Start to move the palms in and out as you breathe, when you bring the palm in it is facing you and when you bring it out it is facing out. Feel the Chi move in and out in your hands. Do this as long as it takes to feel the Chi, play with it. Move more slowly, then faster.

-Wednesday

While sitting rub your hands on your thighs vigorously then stop and hold your palms together, creating Chi. To send that energy to places rub your thighs and place the Chi on your face, then on your heart and anywhere you need some Chi.

-Thursday

Here is a fun game you can play with one or more. I call it Chi ball and use it at the rehabilitation center to get the adolescents interested in yoga. One of you rub your hands together and gather up some Chi then throw the ball to another, playing catch. Try to see if you can see the energy you are throwing. It is fun; your kids will love it. Make up your own rules and games with it. Use this game when you need energy. You can play this alone throwing your Chi ball in the air and catching it.

-Friday

When standing with others today try feeling the Chi around them. You have heard of personal space, that is where your Chi or Aura is. Try expanding yours by visualizing it as big as you want it., then bringing it back in. Play with your Chi.

~ ॐ ~

Weekly Om – Forty

Energy Healing – How to Change Your Energy

Well-being is the result of an unobstructed flow of "Life Energy" around and through the body. Since everything is energy we need energy to be totally connected and to be able to run properly, just like the electronics we use day to day. When you are feeling run down, tired or have no motivation, knowing some energy healing techniques or meditation might do the trick.

Meditating each day you will gain that higher source of energy to help you become stronger. When I am depleted and in need of some energy I like to think of white light coming into my body through the left palm, then seeing and feeling the negative energy leaving though the right. My teachers taught me that energy comes into the left and out the right.

Reiki or Polarity techniques are some other ways of healing your energy. You can learn them yourself or you can find practitioners in your area to work on you.

Reiki is a form of Japanese spiritual healing, meaning Rei (universal) and ki (life energy). A practitioner will draw on the Reiki energy, channeling it to areas of need in themselves and the patients. Reiki acts at an atomic level, causing the body's molecules to vibrate with a higher intensity thus dissolving energy blockages that may lead to disharmony and disease. To be able to channel Reiki yourself you will need to be attuned according to the ancient ways. But once the healing channel is opened in you the Reiki energy can be drawn upon and remain active for life.

Polarity Therapy is a blend of Western Therapies, Chinese Medicine and Ayurvedic practices. Polarity therapists see the body as a system of energy fields and believe that life energy is kept in constant motion by pull of opposing poles, which act like magnets. The head and the right side of the body are positive pole, the feet and the left side are negative poles and the center of the body along the spine and Chakra column are neutral. Energy flows clockwise between the poles passing along the central channel where there are five neutral energy centers of ether, air, fire, water and earth. Illness, poor health and low energy are considered to be the result of depletions and stagnation in these energy centers.

209

I have been taught both these practices and use them everyday, seeing results. Lots of clients will ask afterwards: "what was that you were doing?" They notice some sort of change in their energy field while I am doing the energy healing. Practitioners like myself, may use one or more of these therapies: hands on healing, nutritional advice or exercise, to help restore the energy and bring back balance. Counseling can also be used when practitioners feel that negative thoughts are impeding energy flow. Finding the form of energy healing that fits your needs is up to you, but it can change your life and give you the balance you may need to be at Peace.

Notes:

_____

_____

_____

_____

Energy Healing – Workbook forty

-Monday
Now that you can feel Chi, if you still do not think you can then keep practicing - don't give up! Take that Chi and hold it over areas in the body that need healing. Hold your hands about an inch above that part of the body. Think about sending green energy into this spot. Do this for as long as it takes to feel anything.

-Tuesday
Do Monday's exercise to your pet, child or anyone else. Notice if you feel anything or if they feel better. Use this any time your family members are not feeling well.

-Wednesday
This is called an Earth Balance. It balances out what is under your finger tips.

Take your two hands, thumb and pointer fingers in a square over a part of the body in need of healing. Practice with your knee. Lightly touch and rock back and forth with the fingers. Pick up two opposites, pointer finger and thumb, keep rocking. Then pick up the other. When done lift up and clear your hands by shaking them out.

-Thursday
Do the Chakra Meditation but at the same time hold your right hand over each Chakra as you open and close your petals.

-Friday
Today - all day - clear your energy after meetings, stressful situations and any time you feel it. Clear your hands by taking the thumb and running from pinky finger to pointer fingers and shake out the hands. Then take your hands from head to toe alongside the body clearing the energy out, see it leaving and new energy filling up from head to toe.

~ ॐ ~

Currents of Energy – How do they impact your life?

In past Oms, I talked a bit about two of the four major highways that carry energy currents through the body, the upward current of liberation and the downward current manifestation. When these energy currents are blocked you may have trouble liberating yourself from compulsive behaviors, or creating and manifesting visions in your life. We will discuss more about visualizing and manifesting visions in upcoming weeks.

Within these four major highways there are two horizontal currents that flow. They are called *reception* and *expression*. Within the current called reception you are inwardly receiving information: emotions, love or touch. Through the other you express outwardly what's inside of you like thoughts, creativity or your love. If either of these currents is blocked you may have trouble in social interactions or have difficulty receiving or expressing one or more of the Chakra related aspects.

For example if you can express out, but are not receiving in you are likely to become depleted in one or all of your Chakras. Ever feel drained? Do you give out too much and deplete yourself of energy.

When you are receiving in but cannot express out this will cause any or one of the Chakras to become excessive. It is also possible to become both excessive and deficient in one or all the Chakras.

When becoming excessive or deficient in the Chakras you get stuck in attachment or avoidance. Attachment meaning fixating on something so much that it becomes too important, more important than your regular life or things that you used to love. I tend to look at it like this. If it feels good all the time to be attached to something or someone and you still have time for other activities or have other friends, then it is healthy, but only you can know this.

Avoidance is when you are creating habits of avoiding people or situations. If you tend to want to run from all deep subjects and real relationships, take a look at how you are expressing yourself.

213

One way to keep your energy currents clear is to be conscious of these behaviors, so you can release them by making small changes. Noticing what your behaviors are is the first step to recognizing them. Then take another step forward, speak your truth and use your personal power.

Notes:

_____

_____

Currents of Energy – Workbook forty one

-<u>Monday</u>
Looking at the energy highways list each of the four on separate pieces of paper. Write the names of the highways liberation, manifestation, reception and expression at the top of each page. Make a subtitle called 'Ideas and Thoughts'. On each page list things that would change or happen as a result of these highways being clear.

For example: Title: Liberation; Subtitle: Ideas and Thoughts;
        Freedom from fear, positive change, feeling better, new relationship.

-<u>Tuesday</u>
Take this list of ideas and thoughts; and under each category list what you feel stops you from being clear in these energy currents.

For example: Title: Manifestation; Subtitle: Ideas and Thoughts
        Should feel like little or no effort, more free time, freedom

What blocks:
Negative thoughts, lack of faith, thinking ideas are too big, lack of money or time.

-<u>Wednesday</u>
Take one energy current sheet at a time and work on how you can clear that pathway.

For example: Title: Manifestation

Release worry and negativity, trust that the universe knows what we need, trust in yourself. Get a massage, energy work or acupuncture to clear blocks.

-<u>Thursday</u>
Today remember what you have been working on and make changes. Let go of fear, release negative thoughts and make those appointments.

-<u>Friday</u>
Keep up the good work going forward.

~ ॐ ~

Finding Trust In Yourself – Where is My True Inner Voice?

We have many different voices that speak to us, mainly Spirit and Ego, as they compete for attention. At times it is difficult to know which one to listen to. Sometimes the messages are conflicting and others alluring. We can talk ourselves into anything - even make things sound true and great when they are wrong and unforgivable.

We all have one voice that speaks the truth, encourages us and pushes us to trust in ourselves. This is called our Spirit, higher power or guardian angels. This voice only wants what is best for the Divine purpose.

The ego voice will send you mixed messages to keep you stuck and in conflict. This is the voice of dark patterns, old emotions and bad behaviors. So you see, there are both a devil and an angel sitting on our shoulders. When you listen to the ego voice you may find yourself with power and riches, but you will not have harmonic wealth. One or more of the five elements will be out of balance. You will have struggles and conflicts with no peace in your heart.

Being able to hear clearly your true inner voice and follow it is what brings on this wealth and balance. Your purpose and true path will unfold without struggle.

Your true inner voice is compassionate, loving and is the voice of understanding.

The more you listen and believe this voice, the more the others will fall away and the stronger your true inner voice will become.

Just saying no to the voices that hold judgment or keep you suck in old patterns will help you to stop being critical of yourself. When this behavior ceases the behavior of fear and anger will cease as well. There is abundance for us all, as it is our birthright.

Connecting With the Inner Voice: Meditation
Sitting on your knees, hips towards the heels, stretching your arms out on the floor in front of you, place the forehead against the floor in Childs Pose. Focus on breathing from the belly as you quiet your mind. See if you can quiet yourself enough to hear the truth from your inner voice.

Always remember that sometimes with truth comes disappointment and hurt, but it could be a blessing in disguise. As long as it is giving you encouragement, love and understand keep following it to see what the truth is leading you towards.

Notes:

_____

_____

_____

_____

Finding Trust in Yourself – Workbook forty two

<u>-Monday</u>
Do you believe it is your right to have abundance? _____

If you said yes, and you don't have it, then sit quietly and ask your true voice why you do not have it?

_____

If you said no, sit quietly and ask yourself what makes you believe this way?

_____

Write down anything that comes to you.

_____

_____

_____

<u>-Tuesday</u>
Have you ever let yourself down? _____
Write about why and how?

_____

_____

Look at how you can fix this and follow through so you can trust yourself.

-Wednesday
Do you trust others? Focus on why you do not trust easily. Bring up any past hurt or negative beliefs then do the release meditation and cut the cord to these feelings, opening yourself up to trusting others again. Forgive those who have hurt you and believe that trusting in others and yourself is necessary to being in balance.

_____

_____

-Thursday
Do you believe that your spirit wants the best for you and will guide you on the path of success? _____

If yes, good for you! Focus on what that path is, and start to hear the inner voice expressing how to get there. If not, why do you feel this way?

_____

_____

_____

Say this ten times out loud "Our spirit is on our side and so is the universe. It does not want us to fail." Keep this up until you start to believe it.

<u>-Friday</u>
Do you notice any changes? _____

Are you hearing your true inner voice? _____

Are you listening? _____

Are you trusting? _____

Keep asking yourself this and keep saying plural statements until you notice things changing. Put the statement where you can see it to remind yourself.

_____

_____

_____

_____

~ ॐ ~

Weekly Om – Forty Three

Visualization – Is It the Gift of Power?

Visualization is the ability to use your imagination as a sense. Most think it is a gift and others know it is something we all have the ability to use. We all are born with this ability but if it is not nurtured and used it will fall away and be lost. Not leaving yourself open to the ability, then you will not understand its capability. Feeling like you "can't" or "it's not in your will".

I am here to tell you that it is and you can, it just takes work. I have seen amazing things happen in my life using this ability. I see images in mind's eye of how I want my life, I think about them intensely. Keeping the faith and trusting that it will happen as long as I see it as so, the creative power will make it happen. Just by seeing events, situations, objects in your mind you attract them to you. Seemingly like it's magic but actually it is just the natural process of the power of thought in alignment with the universe.

All successful people use this in a conscious or unconscious way.

Believe me you get what you wish for. If you are always thinking "life is hard" and hating everything then that is the life you will have, just by giving it power by thinking in that manner. If you are fearful and negative, then you expect negative results. You behave, look, and talk accordingly.

Thought is energy, by having certain thoughts in our minds, and by concentrating on them and putting emotional energy into them, they become powerful. These thoughts induce some kind of pressure on the energy fields around us, causing them to move and act. Our thoughts change the balance of energy around us, and in a natural way bring changes in the environment in accordance with the thoughts.

No man that does not see visions will ever realize any high hope or undertake any high enterprise.
--Woodrow Wilson

Being naturally positive in your approach and how you handle situations is what attracts positive results.

Do you want to change your body? If so, next time you get out of the shower try my Body Visualization. If you do not have a full sized mirror, get one now! I started doing this not really understanding what I was doing. I change things by visualization, I understand then how I want it, to see it clearly. Then, before I know it the change appears. I changed my body this way along with changing my diet, simply, as we will discuss later on. I have always loved to move my body, dance and exercise so continuing to do that with the changes made me a new being within about five years. You heard me right, changing your body takes time so give up the scale and thinking it will happen overnight and enjoy your journey. Let's get real here, how long did to take for you to get your body in this state? Then it will take at least half that to get you back. IF you stick to it. If you fall off for a day do not beat yourself up just move on, change is hard we have the old patterns so deeply rooted it might take many tries till you get it right. It's all a journey there is no where to get. Start loving yourself and it will come. If you eat a fairly correct diet then you need more exercise; and if you exercise regularly then you need to look at your eating habits. It's really simple and we make it hard because we are lazy and want the magic pill. THERE IS NO PILL....it takes work. It is easy work if you start to do it. Just change your mind about yourself and the body will follow, it has to. The Law of Attraction is on your side.

Mirror, Mirror -Body Visualization

After a shower or bath, find your full length mirror and stand naked in front of it. Take a good look at your body. If negative thoughts come up say "No", I love this body it is my way through experiencing life. Look at what you would like to change, start with one thing. Pull the skin tight to see what you would like to see and see it! Stare at it imprinting it in your mind. Then go about your day. Do this often and to all the parts of the body you would like to see change.

We spend lots of time in our home space. If you do not feel comfortable, if there is any negativity going on in your home life or you are in a rut then make changes in your space. The changes will then become changes within you and any others with whom you share space.

I was having communication issues with my daughter. Without realizing I decided we were not using the dining room table enough to justify it taking up half the living room. I got rid of the table and created a better sitting area in the living room. I noticed as quickly as I finished putting the room back together the communication breakdown was gone. We feed off the energy in our homes, so if it is cluttered and closed our energy will be also. If the energy is open and flows that is what we will feel. Clean out your closets, organize your space and create your new life.

Room and Home Change Visualization

Sit in the area that you want to change. Start with how you can open it up and create more space. What can you let go of to create the new space. Sit for a bit and let the ideas and possibilities flow. Then each time you are in that space visualize it, and be open to bringing in what you see.

Before you know it, all the items you see will find you and you will think "wow - that is weird".

After I left my abusive relationship and was creating our new home, I got a great paying job. But, I hated going so far every day and being gone from my new place, my growing daughter and my pets for so long. I was traveling 120 miles each day and was gone between ten and twelve hours each day. It so happens that this job came with lunch time yoga classes and I got hooked on doing yoga in the middle of the day. I knew after one week that one day this would be my new job. I took the classes, did the dreaming, and overcame all the doubts and seven years later I am doing all that I love and more. I took time everyday while doing yoga or walking to think about how I wanted to be in the mountains all day, work for myself and do what I love. At times it felt like I would fail at this dream but stopped myself from abandoning it many times.

If you happen to get laid off or lose your job while doing this visualization, be calm and trust in the Divine to bring you what you are asking for. Be careful not to stop the process by becoming afraid of the changes that are happening.

We always need to let go first in order for the new to come, be patient.

Job or Career Change Visualization
What is it you love to do? Breathe as you ask yourself this question. We should love what we do and do what we love. When this answer comes to you then see it when you are in meditation. Take time each day to visualize you in this new job or career even if you have no idea how this will happen. See it then be open and know it will happen. Pay attention to opportunities that arise in the weeks to come.

Notes:

_____

_____

_____

_____

Visualization – Workbook forty three

-Monday
Do the Body Visualization today once in the AM and once in the PM. Add lower light to the PM and really see changes happening.

-<u>Tuesday</u>
Pick a small place or room to try the Room Change Visualization. Do this sometime during your day today. See new colors and have fun decorating in your mind. Draw it if you like that adds more power behind your visualization.

-<u>Wednesday</u>
Do the Body Visualization today once in the AM and once in the PM. Add lower light to the PM and really see changes happening.

-<u>Thursday</u>
If you love your job do the Job Change visualization as a change in something you do not like about your job, or to visualize a promotion or raise. Otherwise, do the visualization as a whole change.

-<u>Friday</u>
Notice what is changing. If nothing yet keep up these visualizations. Make up new ones for other situations like a whole move to another address or other life changes.

~ ॐ ~

Manifesting Visions – Can You Manifest Energy Into Your Reality?

A vision or an inspired idea can motivate you and can push you into action. Have you ever felt the great feeling that anything is possible? When you have clear vision it gets you charged and keeps you going. The very thought fills you with energy and positive feelings. You feel open like anything is possible. These motivate feelings so that you can transform your life.

Some of us have these visions but do not ever manifest them into our reality. How does the excitement and energy that is so positive turn into something negative or nothing at all? Sometimes we let others tell us it is not possible or find out that it will take hard work to achieve it, letting us down thus turning this motivation and positive energy into fear. The fear then blocks the energy's downward flow thus stopping us from manifesting our visions into reality.

Anything **IS** possible; all it takes is the energy to do it. In Om number Four, "The Grounding Experience" I talked about the downward current called _manifestation_. When this current is blocked with fear you cannot manifest any of your visions into reality. The energy cannot come through, it is like blocking a doorway. How do you unblock the doorway? You move! The energy has to be able to move through in order to create the idea into completion. So get past the fear take a step and move that energy into reality.

In the past ten years I have manifested a lot of my thoughts into reality. I have successfully changed my whole being into a new person, my authentic person. I have changed my career and lifestyle. I have built a business from nothing and continue to grow it using only my creative thoughts. There were lots of times I lost faith in the beginning but my spirit is strong and loud, not letting me give up. Stay on the path even when it feels hopeless and recognize when others are negative with your dreams. That is really their own negativity they are projecting.

Don't be afraid of the space between your dreams and reality. If you can dream it, you can make it so.
--Belva Davis

Opening the downward current of Manifestation
Lying on your back focus on your breathing, letting the thoughts pass through you without making judgment or action. Focus on breathing, feeling the belly rise as you inhale and fall as you exhale, focusing on this downward current only. Visualize the energy as white light, coming into the crown and moving through the midline of the body to the feet. If you have a hard time seeing it clearly moving through, then you may have some blockages. Keep working at it until you can see the energy moving freely through the downward current.

Opening up this channel of energy will allow you to begin to co-create in harmony with the Divine will.

Notes:

_____

_____

_____

_____

Manifesting Visions – Workbook forty four

-Monday
First you have to know what your vision is. Once you have that, ask yourself how much focus do you give this vision? Do you spend time thinking about it; what it will look like and how you will need it to be? If not, start today setting aside time to sit with your visions.

_____

-Tuesday
Do the 'Opening the downward current of Manifestation' meditation today as much as you can.

-Wednesday
Have any possibilities arisen? Notice how your energy feels.

_____   _____   _____

Take time today to focus on your dreams and visions of your life for at least fifteen minutes. Think of your dreams while in the shower, eating lunch alone or while you exercise. Turn off the TV and watch your visions instead.

-Thursday
Before bed tonight take time to write what your visions are.

_____   _____   _____

-Friday
Make a Vision Board.   ...
Get a poster board, some glue and scissors.

Find all the magazines in your home and start to pull out pages that you like. You can glue words, pictures and sentences glue them onto the poster board.

Let your intuition guide you and try not to think or plan how to do this.

If you are having a hard time, put it down and meditate for a bit first.

Try not to be in your head while making your board.

Then when it's completed hang it somewhere you can see it.

~ ॐ ~

Yoga – How Does Yoga Help Your Health?

I have been teaching yoga for five years now. When I began I was overweight and inflexible. I can remember being in a crossed legged position, with my teacher asking us to fold forward. When she said have a straight back, I realized I was uncomfortable and was not able to fold very far. Years later, in this pose I can reach the ground and I am very comfortable. Being flexible is also something we all can possess. A healthy muscle is one that is both strong and flexible. I feel yoga is a bit misunderstood and most are afraid of trying it. It is just stretching and exercise, you can do it because it is not about being number one while doing it. Yoga has no competition behind it. I tell my class do not think you have to look like me or the person next to you, it's about what your body can do and being with your breath.

The word "yoga" meaning union can be understood as a comprehensive approach to healing, as it goes right to the root of all disease. Most of the diseases are the symptoms of an underlying dis-ease that has been prolonged and turned into a real disease. When we are ill or feeling dis-ease, our bodies fall out of balance. Becoming out of balance the energy does not circulate freely within us, and becomes stuck in that body part causing a real illness.

When we are experiencing the 'out of balance mode' is when we should be doing yoga, meditating or some type of bodywork to help bring us back in balance. We should be watching our eating habits at these times as well. When you are ill or in dis-ease you have thoughts of not wanting to take care of yourself or wanting to just be still. This is not how our bodies are designed. We need to move the unhealthy energy out and being still just prolongs it from moving. Although rest is good to help the healing process, recognizing the difference between resting to heal and enabling your dis-ease is key!

Being in balance is a scary place for people. We have gotten used to being stressed out, worrying about life instead of living it. Being in conflict and having difficulty has become a comfort to us. On some level we even enjoy our pain as we use it as an excuse to get out of living. It takes work to get there but when you do it's a great place to be - living in the present moment!

What if we can skillfully redirect our efforts to making a change? Would we then liberate ourselves and untrap a resource of energy within? I know so! I have been there and now I am on the other side of discomfort. I have been in hate with myself and not comfortable in my body. I have done the redirecting and the clearing of blocks and now say with confidence that I love myself and feel totally comfortable with and in my body. This was mostly achieved by doing yoga.

I love the balance poses in Yoga - Tree, Warrior Three and Dancers pose. To stay balanced on one leg you need to focus on something, the focus is what holds you in place, using a different resource of energy and redirecting your internal energy to something different. This rewires the brain for a more positive reaction.

__Tree Pose__ – Rocking from heel to toes, finding that spot where you feel centered and grounded then focusing on a spot in front of you creating balance in the body. Taking one leg and placing it on your calf or inner thigh and bringing the hands together in front of the heart. Breathing, focusing and balancing. See if you can bring your hands above your head. Hold this pose as long as you can balance. Repeat other side.

__Warrior Three__ – Glide the leg back, bringing the arms up aligning them with the ears. Back leg floats up as you bring the torso and arms down reaching long. Breathing, focusing and balancing as long as you are able. Repeat other side.

__Dancers Pose__ – Taking your right foot in your right hand, bring it to your hip, the left arm aligns with the ear same as in Warrior Three, torso and arm move down and reach long. Right leg presses up and back at the same time. Breathing, Focusing and balancing as long as you are able. Repeat other side.

Find a teacher, class or DVD that fits your needs and go for it... stretch that body - or you can find this exercise in my "Groovy Goddess Workout" DVD.

__Notes:__

_____

_____

_____

Balance Studio 20 Minute Home Workout
Sun Salutation

Mountain Pose

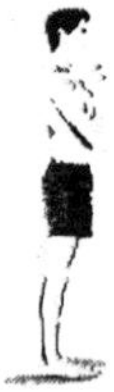

#1

Hands to sky

Swan dive down
with palms turned
out (flat back)

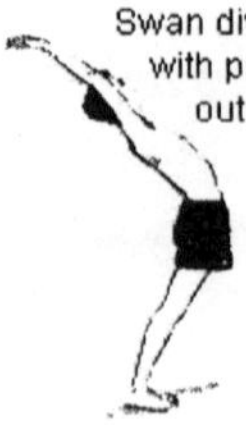

#2

Forward bending (folding at the hips)

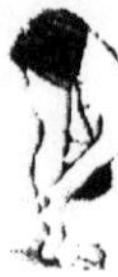

#3

Lunging

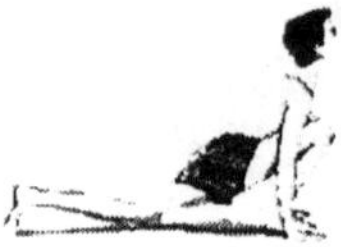

#4

Downward facing dog

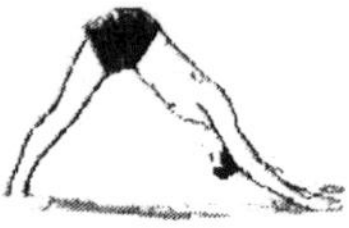

#5

Plank pose (push up pose)

Yoga push up

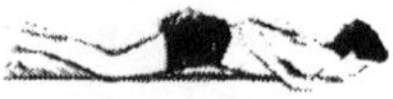

#6

**(drop knees,
think chest to floor before stomach)**

Cobra pose

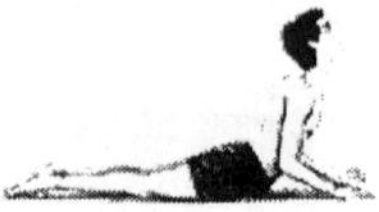

#7

Downward facing dog

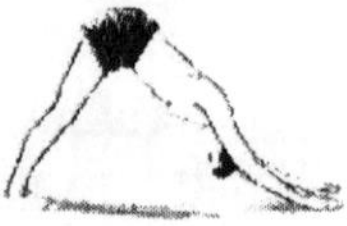

#8

Lunging opposite side

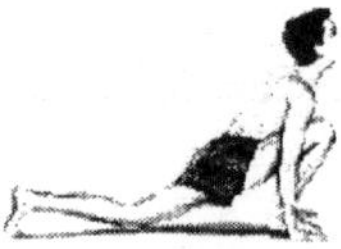

#9

Forward bending (folding at the hips)

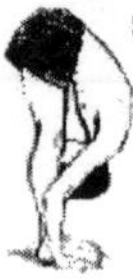

Swan dive up
with palms turned
up (flat back)

#10

Hands to sky

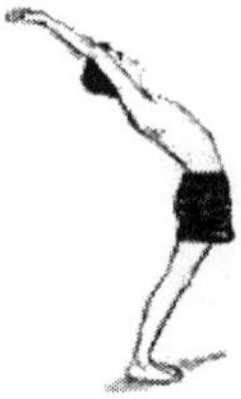

#11

Mountain Pose with hands in Namaste

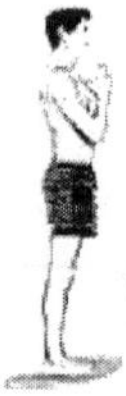

#12

repeat 2 times

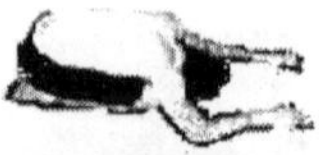

**On last Sun salutation
move to childs pose**

Yoga – Workbook forty five

-Monday
Do one of the Sun Salutation sessions before you start your day.

-Tuesday
Do two of the Sun Salutation sessions today.

-Wednesday
Find more yoga stretches online and do them today.

-Thursday
Do three of the Sun Salutation sessions today, and do some stretches each time; repeat each time today you find yourself waiting in a line. My favorite waiting in line stretches are: neck rolls, shoulder rolls and forward bends, or just being present.

-Friday
Do you notice changes? Flexibility comes fast. Keep moving and trying to stretch all day.

_____   _____   _____

At your desk remember to stretch your hands and wrists. Stand up and place your hands on the desk then turn the fingers tips facing you.

~ ॐ ~

Food - Are We What We Eat?

We all grew up hearing "Eat a balanced meal", but what is that? I agree it is confusing what information or diet we should follow. What I do know is that our bodies need food to run properly. We hear that obesity and type-two diabetes are on the rise and this is mainly due to the bad carbohydrate and sugar intake. These types of foods keep us hungry for more and addicted... like a drug.

I have noticed a change in my cravings in the last couple of years. I now crave veggies and dislike the smell of fast food when that was all I used to crave. I once read that your plate should have all the colors of the rainbow. I started there, by making sure my plate was full of colorful food, leafy greens, purple cabbage, orange carrots, red radishes and so on.

Then I looked at my portion sizes and cut in ½ the carbohydrates (carbs) on my plate and a bit of the proteins I was eating. I told myself to eat veggies and salads first to get them out of the way. Then I would reward myself with the rest. I took a look at my soda intake, which was too much! I created a boundary of one a day at lunch and the same for my sweet intake. This I could live with! No more yo-yo dieting, no more starving myself and no more trying to follow any type of food program. I eat what I want when I want as long as it's balanced. I wrote this four years ago and now can say I am off soda completely and better at my eating habits even still.

We are what we eat.
If we are eating healthy and balanced,
that is exactly what we will be.
--Melissa Stone

To gain the wisdom and healing power of whole, natural foods try this visualization exercise.

Healthy Eating Meditation

Sitting in a comfortable position inhale and exhale through the nose a couple of times, allowing yourself to completely relax. In your mind's eye see your plate as it is now. Start to notice the colors and seeing if it looks like is it a healthy plate. Now meditate on the changes you would like to make start to incorporate healthy foods. Focus on one veggie you may not like, try smelling it as it is cooking. tasting it in your mouth and liking it.

Notes:

_____

_____

_____

Food - Workbook forty six

-Monday

Are you what you eat? Make a list of everything you eat today.

_____	_____	_____
_____	_____	_____
_____	_____	_____
_____	_____	_____

Notice how you are eating, is it healthy or not? _____

-<u>Tuesday</u>
Add in more veggies today, at least for one meal.

-<u>Wednesday</u>
Take out all sugars today and keep the veggies in.

-<u>Thursday</u>
Go through your cupboards today and get rid of all processed food, sweets and sodas.

-<u>Friday</u>
Make a contract with yourself to start eating healthy, no more diets, just focus on healthy eating.

~ ॐ ~

Like A Song – How We Create Intentions

Looking at our lives, personalities and emotions, we are so many things all at once. We are parents, co-workers, life partners and children to name a few, all in one physical body. I feel like I wear different hats all day. One minute I am a yoga teacher, then a massage therapist, a writer, a gardener, a house cleaner and a mother all in one day.

People ask me which one would you choose to be all day if you could. I say I like it now just the way it is. I have great balance in all that I do and I love it all.

It is like a song with different tracks all meshing together telling a story, my story that I then share with the world creating positive change. When writing a piece of music or creating a song you need to lay down the foundation. You create the rest by laying down one track at a time, each instrument and each vocal separately, but as one together. This is done in hopes that it will bring together what you were feeling when you began the journey or creating the song. I feel my journey is in harmony with my song and I can sing freely and with confidence that all the instruments and words are in order, the order of change for the positive.

What journey do you want to be on? Are you creating the foundation and all the tracks that you need so that it will all mesh together the way you intended? Or are you creating situations, ideas and emotions to make it look one way to others when in reality it's not. If one instrument is out of tune or if your vocals are not in key, the song will not sound appealing. Is your body out of tune? Are you in the right key? Tune into your own music or that of the world around you.

Sing like no one's listening, love like you've never been hurt, dance like nobody's watching, and live like its heaven on earth.
--Mark Twain

The Ocean is a great place for meditating on the sounds of nature. Even if you live in the city there is music to be heard all around if you just let go and listen. Listen to the wind howl, the sounds of the cars rushing by, or the rain hitting the roof.

Tuning into these sounds might help you to create your own song taking you on the journey of your real intention.

Notes:

_____

_____

_____

Like a Song – Workbook forty seven

-Monday
How is your life like a song? Write about what is the foundation of your life or song.

_____

_____

What are the instruments or things that make up your journey?

-Tuesday
How can you attune to these in a more positive way?

_____

_____

-Wednesday
What are the sounds of song around you? Make a list of them tonight, noticing all day what the sounds are in your life. How do they make up your song?

_____ _____ _____

_____ _____ _____

_____ _____ _____

_____ _____ _____

-Thursday
Try to write lyrics to your own song. Even if it sounds silly keep writing. Have fun with it.

-<u>Friday</u>
Finish and sing your song out loud to yourself, have fun and laugh. Create music in your head or play an instrument to your song.

~ ॐ ~

Currency – What Does Money Have to Do With It?

When searching the web for the meaning of currency, you will only find information about money. Is it always about the money? Would the Worlds' focus change if we looked at currency it in a new and different way? Currency is a way to exchange something for goods.

Everything is energy! This being the truth then can't an exchange of energy be currency as well? Meaning that if you offer something other than money it is still a trade of something for goods. It is done in the business world all the time. Being an apprentice at a firm or being a teacher's aide. It's not for the money that you take the job, it's for the experience.

If we look at currency in whole like this, then we see that we can have anything we desire. Walking through life being open minded and social you meet others and opportunities arise. When you are listening to what they have to offer and are open to it, you might notice that you have something to offer them as well. You will see that the universe is bringing you everything you want and need, and it's the same for them.

This happens to me all the time, now that I understand how the laws of attraction work.

I just have to have a clear vision of what I want, state it to others and meditate on it. Then, without having the money for it, somehow weeks or months later I realize I have it.

All you need to do is ask and appreciate what is already been set forth. With patience, guidance and most of all trust let worries of money fall away! Allow only thoughts of appreciation and living your life as your true authentic self should.

Focus on your gifts and let your intuition flow. Life will hand you what you need to fulfill your dreams as long as you keep appreciating and trusting in the Divine purpose.

Sometimes I fall off this wagon but it does not take me long to get back on. When I look around I appreciate all that I have achieved, with little or no money. I used to think money was evil, that it caused others to become power hogs and be egotistical. Now I understand it is just a means to exchange and those that use it for power and no good are just out of balance. Money can be used for good in the right hands, but it is not the only means. Our minds are what really bring us our dreams. Set yours to being open and balance out your energy so the abundance can flow.

Notes:

_____

_____

_____

Currency – Workbook forty eight

-Monday
Take a look at how you see money. Is it the only means to getting what you want?

_____   _____   _____

Do you think that if you had more money you would live better, feel better about yourself or have peace? Why?

_____

-Tuesday
Today appreciate all the money you have in your possession and any given to you today. Then all day long as you give money away say to yourself I know this is well spent and giving this away will help others, and then come back to me as more.

-<u>Wednesday</u>
Give some money to someone that needs it today.

-<u>Thursday</u>
Think of something that you can offer someone else and think of something someone else can give you and ask them for a trade. Notice how great this works with no exchange of currency.

-<u>Friday</u>
Today give some money to someone that needs it.

~ ॐ ~

Truth Of Impermanence - What is Dharma?

I do not watch too much TV and this is why I can accomplish much more than most. When I do sit down to watch it I love shows that will still teach me about what I love, and that is life itself. My favorite TV show was and can still be seen in rerun form: 'Dharma and Greg'. This show was accurate in showing how to live in balance. Dharma, a yoga Instructor married to a rich lawyer, was not affected by material wealth, power or everyday situations.

When we encounter difficulty, we often ask; Why me? What did I do to deserve this? We look at all of life from our own personal viewpoint, seeing ourselves as fixed features in a world fraught with all kinds of bodily harm and unexpected danger. Even as we grow older, we worry about the inevitable changes our body encounters, feeling old and that life is passing us by.

The fact is that life is endless; you have the power to stop this physical life from passing you by and from feeling old. Human beings cause their own suffering when they consider their egos to be fixed and permanent and therefore at conflict with a world of change. Instead, we should awaken to Dharma, the truth of impermanence.

The term Dharma has come to refer to a number of concepts including truth, virtue, teachings and Nirvana. Dharma always means the change that occurs when we awaken to the true nature of our lives and the greatest possible good. This ultimate state is reached when we have rooted out the causes of our self-centered dissatisfaction. We can achieve this by having a healthy mentality state of being, which is another meaning for the term Dharma. In order to acquire this virtuous mentality, we have to be willing to learn and be open to change.

I walk in balance on the path of truth.
--Unknown

Dharma is also used to refer to teachings. Any teachings that help you reach a state of compassion can be considered Dharma. The word Dharma can be a helpful guide on a quest for enlightenment. By opening our minds to the teachings around us, we begin to embody a new, healthy mentality. Our teachers may come in the form of a family member, advisor or piece of writing, but we may also find a guide within ourselves. By awakening to the truth of our interdependence we become far more than individuals struggling. We embody truth.

Notes:

_____

_____

Truth of Impermanence - Workbook forty nine

-Monday
What is your truth? Focus on thinking this, what comes to mind?

_____   _____   _____

_____   _____   _____

_____   _____   _____

-Tuesday
Continue writing down your truths; are there parts of you that you are not being truthful with yourself about?

_____   _____   _____

_____   _____   _____

-Wednesday
Make a list of how can you make your life whole and full of truth?

_____   _____

_____   _____

_____   _____

_____   _____

-Thursday
Tell only truth today.

-Friday
How has your life been changing, and notice what truths have been appearing since you started reading this book and doing the exercises.

_____   _____

_____   _____

_____   _____

_____   _____

~ ॐ ~

Giving – How The Little Gifts Spread Joy

If you have been reading these Oms weekly beginning in January, then reading this now we are in full holiday season. If not, then mark your calendar to re-read this during the year-end holiday season. These next two Oms were written because of the holiday stress I feel and see each year.

I have stopped getting stressed over presents, decorating and parties. Over the last couple of years I have decided it is not worth the damage to my body. If the decorating does not get done then I will enjoy others decorations. If the perfect present is not found, then I will give something of a much greater use, like my time or love. If I cannot make it to a party, it's not the end of the world.

In order for there to be a harmonious world there needs to be the giving of ourselves. When we think of giving we tend to think in the sense of money or material goods. There is much more out there to give that can be valued at a higher level, giving of yourself – your time, your emotions and your energy.

Take time everyday to give back to the Earth and our loved ones everyday, not just during the holiday season. Perhaps picking up a piece of litter will give back to the earth and our community. I had the privilege of teaching Physical Education (PE) to 5th and 6th graders one school year. I asked kids to help keep the school clean by picking up litter because our PE games were outside amongst the litter. I was shocked by the response I would get. They would tell me "that is not mine." Or "I don't want to." Even my daughter tells me this at times. It does not matter because it is all ours to take care of. When walking anywhere if there is some garbage in your path, pick it up and take it to the closest garbage receptacle. It makes you feel good and keeps our community clean. It inspires others around to do the same.

Helping someone in need or giving someone a much-needed hug gives back to our community as well. When I see anyone struggling I ask to help. I once saw this older lady struggling to put groceries in her car. I asked, "Did she need help?" She was shocked I cared enough; I helped her and could see the gratefulness in her eyes. It took just minutes to help her, I probably made her day and I felt great in doing so. I have lots of these stories; I feel it is my duty as a human being on this Earth to help others. I help older people, hurt people and kids in need. I give my time freely but at the same time I am in control of it as to not give away my power with the help.

The universe gives us opportunity everyday all day long to give back and in return the universe gives us abundance or Karma in Blessing form. Karma is given for everything we do whether it is good or bad and sometimes can be in the form of Blessings in disguise or lessons. It takes a connected being to realize the potential of this. When realized it can seem like life just hands you all your dreams. Within this PEACEFUL place you will always find more than money could ever buy! When you are down and out the best way to boost yourself back up is to do something for someone or for our planet. Start today by only putting

Do a good deed, pay it forward
--Melissa Stone

good positive energy out into the world by feeling unconditional love for all that roam this planet with us. Let's pick up after each other, not hate each other and be positive role models for our kids. Releasing all that is negative will bring peace, love and understanding into your world. Then it will spill over and inspire all the lives that you touch.

When you look at it in this sense, does it not give you purpose? Thinking in terms of "If I miss this opportunity I might cause others to miss one as well" you get the feeling of your importance in life. Isn't that what we all are looking for? We don't need to know the meaning of life we just need to live it for all that it is worth. Take all the opportunities not looking for payoff but knowing that in return it will all happen just like you dream when it's for the good of all!

<u>*Notes:*</u>

_____

_____

_____

_____

Giving – Workbook fifty

-<u>Monday</u>
Make a point today to pick up any litter you see and to help anyone struggling.

At the end of the day make a list of what you did and how much time it took. How did this make you feel today?

_____   _____

_____   _____

_____   _____

_____   _____

-<u>Tuesday</u>
Take a look at your holiday gift list.

Are you able to pay cash for it all? If not, make a new list that gives gifts of time and or things that you can pay cash for. Do you draw, write or bake? Give gifts that are from love instead of making you more in debt.

-<u>Wednesday</u>
This time of year all charities are asking for cash donations and it's hard to be able to give to them all. Do you have a change jar? If so, divide up the change and donate that.

If you do not but feel you want to do something, do a meditation of giving to them all.

See yourself being able to give to them, see others being able to give. Then send these charities white light, green energy and joy.

-<u>Thursday</u>
Do you know someone that needs some love? Someone in your office, school or neighborhood, send them a note or small gift. I love to give these rocks that have words on them like bless, healing or love. Tell them they are worth love and peace and that you care.

-<u>Friday</u>
Give yourself some love today. Find some time to sit quietly and feel the love all around you. See and feel the joy of living.

After you finish this book, give it to someone that may need it or send them a new copy.

~ ॐ ~

Customer Service – Are We Giving Customer Service All The Time?

This is what I do best, give customer service. I do want it from others, but find myself wondering "What has happened to good customer service?" Being a manager in a corporate setting for the first twenty years of my career. I have taken a lot of customer service training classes. I feel I give excellent customer service to everyone. You see everyone is our customer and if we look it in this light we might all be better at it.

In any customer service training course you will hear this statement "The customer is always right!" This is because it is their experience and how they feel. Giving excuses, being defensive or even agreeing cannot change how they feel until they have released it and are ready to. The goal is to find the best solution for all. Making eye contact, listening and being there for them is what customer service is all about, being empathetic to their situation and needs. Then giving problem solving solutions, letting them decide which is best for them to let go of the issue.

I see less and less of this in places of business. Perhaps we have also lost these values in our daily lives well? The customer does not have to just be an individual that pays you money for a service. It can be anyone, as we are all making some sort of exchange any time we have interactions with one another. Exchange of energy, ideas, material possessions or cash, it's all an exchange that can be positive or negative. When the exchange is not positive for one of the parties it will cause the imbalance to happen.

The unhappy party might not say anything to you; they might feel more comfortable telling a close friend of the situation. Venting their frustrations, to say the problem out loud is a way to help process the issue and keep it from being stored in their body. What is at risk is giving this frustration to others as you vent. If the issue were solved with excellent customer service no one would have to vent anger. Their story would then be about how positive the situation became, making you the customer service hero.

Venting is a way to release the energy of your anger or frustration. When you feel someone is venting make sure to put on your protection bubble of white light around you and let them say what needs to be said. You can help after listening by asking them if they would like to hear a possible solution. Give only positive solutions or ways they can let it go.

Never take on someone's venting! Hear what someone has to say, being open to it but not taking it on and then storing it in your body. If it starts to make you feel overwhelmed or stressed you are taking it on. At that point take in a deep breath and remember that it is not your problem. You are just there to help someone feel better and that should make you feel better. We should be helping each other in healing our wounds not stressing each other out.

Remembering that our customers are our neighbors, friends, family members, colleges, class mates, people in our community and most of all the people we love.

Let's get back to giving the best customer service possible to everyone we encounter in order to keep Peace around us.

Venting Breathing Meditation
Sitting in a chair, breathe from the belly. As you inhale the belly raises and as you exhale the belly falls. Placing your hands on your thighs take in a deep long inhale through the nose and exhale out five short quick breaths. Feel the compression in the belly as you exhale out. Visualize the issue or emotion leaving as you exhale the quick breaths.

Do this until you feel the energy clearing from your body. If need be do one of the cleansing or releasing rituals that we have already discussed.

Notes:

_____

_____

_____

_____

Customer Service – Workbook fifty one

-Monday
Make a list of excellent customer service you have given or received.

~ Notice what made it excellent, keep this in your mind at all times and give it out to someone today.

-Tuesday
Make a list of those to whom you have not given excellent customer service. What can you do to change this? If you can, change it now and only give them excellent customer service going forward.

-Wednesday
Make a list of who your customers are; such as neighbors, friends and family.

_____   _____

_____   _____

_____   _____

Make a list of those that you could give better service to.

_____   _____

_____   _____

-Thursday
List out ideas on how you can give better customer service to those on your list.

_____   _____

_____   _____

_____   _____

_____   _____

-<u>Friday</u>
How has your customer service changed this week? How have others changed around you because of these changes?

_____ _____

_____ _____

_____ _____

_____ _____

_____ _____

_____ _____

~ ॐ ~

Weekly Om – Fifty Two

Living With Spirit - How to Be At Peace

This is the last of the fifty two Weekly Oms I wrote, creating one year of spiritually inspirational passages that will hopefully give enlightenment to those who read them. You are ready to live with your spirit, having now the wisdom of living in the present moment and knowing that it is all just energy. The ultimate challenge is that of living in spirit in a material world, being in balance every day.

You should now have some idea of how energy works within the physical body, emotional body and central nervous system (Chakras). Because everything is made up of energy, it takes work to change and everything is a lesson to be learned. When all else fails keep reminding yourself that everything happens for a reason. If you wait in patience instead of reacting you may see this at the end of the story.

The art to living a Peaceful life is to always remember that when others are in negativity, send them love, and when you are in negativity, have a support group of others that will do the same for you. You are worth the work it takes to be at peace. There is a purpose for your pain and you can get yourself through it.

When you hurt someone... make it right as soon as the emotions calm down, in order to keep your karma clear. If they will not forgive you then forgive them. If they should not be involved in clearing the issue, do it for yourself to clear it energetically. Use the releasing meditation, and other releasing practices mentioned throughout this book.

If we all were conscious of turning the negative energy into positive energy would we then have peace? Learn the lessons and change the outcome into positive reality, and life will become easy for us all. You would without thought start to make different choices creating ideas, opportunities and your path. It will all begin to take on its own form and flow from your being, just as writing these Oms have for me. You will find yourself being in balance.

I live and create in the moment
--Unknown

269

I hope I have helped you in some way with my insight to the metaphysical world as I see and know it to be.

Notes:

_____

_____

_____

Living With Spirit – Workbook fifty two

-Monday
Make a list out of all that you have realized by reading these Oms.

_____   _____

_____   _____

_____   _____

-Tuesday
Make a list of how this new attitude has changed your life or given you opportunities.

_____   _____

_____   _____

_____   _____

-Wednesday
How can you put this to good use in helping others?

_____   _____

_____   _____

_____   _____

-Thursday
Start to think of how many lives you have touched and see how you can be the change in the world that you want to see.

-Friday
Make these lists and ponderings into a comment on how this book helped you and send it to me Melissa@balancestudio.org

_____

_____

_____

_____

_____

~ ॐ ~

The Last Om

Death – Is It Really the End?

I did not write this at the same time as the other Oms. This was not ready to be written until now, as I write and complete my book. There will not be a workbook on death, but maybe a suggestion. That when you are faced with death, either a loved one or yourself, to be open to the work of the universe and the journey it will bring forth.

I now understand that death is not the end and not the beginning either, it is part of a continuum, a circle if you will. I know this from these experiences I am about to tell you about.

I have already expressed in the introduction about my first experience with death. My grandmother, someone very dear to me was dying and I was not made a part of it. It was hidden from me because I was 'too young to understand'. Or was it that it was too hard for the adults to explain?

I would live a lot of years after this without death touching my life, until about age nineteen, when a woman I used to baby sit for was dying of Cancer. She was a mother like figure to me, but when I was asked to her bedside to say goodbye I could not do it. I said I would be there but never went.

My point in these two stories is when we are so afraid of death we lose the experience of it. It is part of life and as sad as it is we need to feel it, to be a part of it so it can be a loving beautiful experience.

I would go though my twenties not really being affected by death until my best friend Sally's dad died. He had a long and hard battle with heart disease from as far back as our friendship. Again I could not bring myself to see it, but I felt this one. The moment he died, I was miles away in my own home. I can remember starting to cry, my husband at the time said "What is going on?" I said, "I am not sure." Within the hour the phone rang and I got the news. I believe because he loved me like a daughter he said goodbye even though I was not there and I felt it, not really knowing what it was until I was told.

The next set of deaths would change me forever. In December of 2003 my best friend Sally was here helping me in create my yoga studio. The phone rang and it was her husband. He told us Sergio, her cousin, had died the night before. We could not believe it, he was only thirty five. How could this happen? I remember we did a small ceremony for him in my studio that night. Sergio could put a smile on anyone's face by saying hello. I can still see him saying "Hi Missi" (my nickname) and whatever mood I was in would go away, from the big smile on his face and joy in his voice.

I called my other good friend Kathy, to tell her. Years earlier she had moved to the country about three hours away thinking it would help her aliments. In my eyes she was just a victim of stress and western medicine gone bad; too many surgeries, prescription medications and pain killers. I called her every day the last three years of her life, sometimes more than once. When I enrolled in massage school and learned energy work. I would drive up just to give her some. Each time I went, I felt her energy leaving her body; my intuition was telling me she was dying. I told her of Sergio's passing. Three days later she called me saying 'I want to stay with you after the holidays. Help me, because I can't do this anymore.' I was excited maybe I could get some healers to help bring her back to the Kathy I once knew. The next day I called and there was no answer, she was gone. I did not find out until the day after and it was the most devastating thing that ever hit me. She was right, she could not do it anymore! I did not know what to do, all I could so was to cry. I would now have two funerals to go to for two people I loved dearly, with both being under forty. At this time I was still working a full time job and getting ready to open my studio. The day after I was told about Kathy's passing, I was driving to work and I remember driving really bad and fast. Crying and thinking to myself I need to calm down or something bad will happen to me. At that moment I pulled off the side of the road and parked in this beautiful spot off Highway 9, overlooking the redwoods. I could not calm myself down and could not stop crying. Then something stopped me, I heard "I am ok, it is ok." I thought I was hearing things but it was Kathy's voice. Then as I looked in the sky I could see her face. It looked like the ending of the movie, Van Helsing. I shook my head and said to myself this is crazy. I should remind you that I truly believe in spirits and the metaphysical world. I just had never experienced this so I could not believe it was really happening. I also noticed that I started to feel calm and at peace. I could think clearly and it was ok. I said I love you and I will miss you and she said she had to go and was gone. This was just the first of many experiences that week.

At both funerals people talked about meeting angles during this time of grief and having dreams of them saying goodbye. These stories were happening to others as well. This was an amazing experience I wanted to feel and know. It was the holiday season and I was feeling like it was truly going to be one filled with love, faith and miracles.

The day of Kathy's wake I was getting lunch at the market. When I met three very spiritual people; I can only describe them as angels with the bluest eyes I

274

have ever seen. The three kind of all looked alike, two females and one male. This was the most amazing experience for me. I went to this store to get food for a friend. He was the cousin to Kathy's husband and I went to offer condolences and found him in depression. I could not even see his soul. I thought I should feed him and help him get to the wake that night. I was waiting in line for food, I turned to pick up a drink and turned back to face the counter. As I did this, something fell. I went back and picked up the three bags of cookies that fell. When I did this I noticed the holes were ripped like they were pulled off. I certainly did not pull them off. Puzzled, I put them back and turned to the three and said, "Sorry, I knocked those off." The older of the two women, said to me "No honey you did not do that, the ghost did." I had to think a minute, and then turned to her and told her that it was funny she should say that today as two people in my life recently died. She was confident in telling me that it was my girl friend that knocked off the cookies to get my attention and that she will be with me like promised until after the holidays. As I drove home I realized Kathy had dropped the cookies as a real sign. You see, the last time she visited me we went shopping and she was putting all these cookies and sweets in the cart and I was taking them all out. I was trying to help her get her eating back on track. We got in a huge fight that night. She was so strung out on pain killers she fell asleep in the cupcakes on the drive home. Her soul knew I loved her and was trying to help her but her ego and addictions were taking over her body. It was sad! She realized I was trying to help her, but it was too late. We made up and then I saw her once more before her death. The week of Thanksgiving the year before she died is my fondest memory and time with her. Dropping the cookies was the sign she was connecting with me. In our twenty year friendship Kathy was the only friend that I would talk to about all of my metaphysical experiences and explorations. I remember one phone conversation when I was about 21 with Kathy about out of body experiences; I had just learned how to do this. Basically I taught myself Transcendental meditation (TM). We always said we would try to connect after death and the cookie dropping was yet another connection with me and confirmation that we do not die and go away. She is just energy now, I still feel her and talk with her all the time - it is just different. She still calms me when I need it most and I still hear her say "You are doing a good job."

The last sign or event with these two deaths is the fact they did not know each other, but somehow are buried next to each other in the same cemetery. I did find it odd that they were both laid to rest in the same cemetery after the funerals, but a month later. To our surprise Sally and I went to put flowers on their graves we noticed they are buried next two each other. Wow, that must mean something. They actually would have liked each other, Sergio was so carefree and fun to hang out with. He always made me smile and it was always an adventure to be around him. Kathy was also fun, we used to dance, play card games and talk all night when she was well. I hope they know each other now and have fun. Sometimes I think they play tricks on me hiding stuff around my house, for me to find back in the same places I looked earlier.

Three years later, I would get the opportunity to talk to Dannion Brinkley, author of three books based on his deaths. You read this right he has died three times. December 17 2007, Sophy and I on our radio show were interviewing him. On air I started to talk about Sergio and Kathy being buried next to each other and what I felt it meant. He talked about it and confirmed my feelings. You can listen to the show on my web-site. The best part is when I got in the car I realized this day was the three year anniversary of Kathy's death. This proves to me there is a bigger picture and the universe does have a plan and it is divine. When I booked Dannion I did not realize what day I had booked him on and I had not planned on bringing up this subject of their death. I wanted to talk about his death experiences. See when you follow your inner guidance and spirit things just happen and it is magic and are all miracles. My life unfolds like a well written movie as events all are with meaning and the power of my intentions. When you live like that how can death be a bad thing?

This story is amazing and it is one of watching the journey of death unfold; it certainly did teach me a lot about love of family and the journey of death. But, first I would like to mention that as I write this on July 25, 2008, I will learn of the passing of Randy Pausch, hearing his name just months before while getting a pedicure, as I watched him on Oprah in the salon. I could only hear bits and pieces of the show over all the talking but found myself almost in tears of joy, listening to him discuss how his dying would teach others. Many, many kudos to you Randy, and many blessings to you as well. You are an inspiration to us all that death is a part of life and if we make the best of life death is not the end and not without purpose.

One day in March, this vibrant goddess came to one of my Pilates classes. After class she explained why she was here in the San Lorenzo Valley. Originally from Malibu, CA, Missy was moving here temporarily to either help her daughter beat the cancer battle or to help her through the journey of death. A mother of four daughters, her 39 year old, Parrish had brain cancer. It had been in remission for 6 years, but was back with a vengeance. I met Parrish in May 2007, when she came for a detox treatment. When I saw her I knew she was an angel, she was so beautiful...too beautiful to be dying. I had such high hopes for her to overcome this, as I am sure the family did as well. At first it looked hopeful the tumor was getting smaller, but then the next MRI a couple of months later would reveal its growth spurt. I would give her a couple of massages and during would pray and visualize the tumor getting smaller, but God had plans for this angel. One afternoon I got a phone call from Missy, Parrish had been given thirty days and would I come weekly to help them all cope? I was honored to be a part of this, but scared at the thought of watching this wonderful being loose all her energy.

I had not been a part of any of the deaths that touched me in the past. How would I handle this? I understood the great opportunity at hand and took the journey. Each week I made the trip to where they wanted me to go to give healing and peace to Parrish and the family. The first place was a beach house they rented for her last vacation with her boyfriend and her friends to visit. Parrish was in and out of her body that day and could not stay still. She was having a hard time speaking and I was helping them all understand what she was feeling by being in touch with her energy and expressing what she was feeling through my voice. This was not the first time I had felt what another was feeling but the first time I would speak for someone else. When this happens I feel so close to God (spirit) and can feel so much energy running through me. I feel at peace and I feel like I am watching someone else, like it is not me but something much higher channeling through me. It is an amazing feeling and I feel blessed to be able to go to this place. She was having a hard day and I felt like I was able to communicate what she was feeling to the others that were there. I gave her boyfriend a massage and felt his anger over letting her go. I could feel how much he loved her and how he did not want her to go. Everyone was feeling this way. I cried the whole drive home.

The next time I would see Parrish she would be bed ridden and not able to speak. When I walked up to her bed I could see in her eyes she knew I was there and I could see her talking to me through her eyes. Her family was all there and they had been busy doing mosaic art, picture collages, healing rituals and anything creative to help make the most out of this negativity.

This is the best experience of "letting go" and "unconditional love" I have ever felt or been able to experience. They did not want to but they were letting the universe do its Divine purpose. They had no expectations and were letting God be the one in control. They were saying "yes" to God and were being Parrish's guides so she could make her journey to the other side, which she did on September 9, 2007 (the day after my daughter turned 13), two days after I saw her last. I remember them all showing me poems, songs and her last writings. I remember the love of a family letting go of their precious Par Par. When I said goodbye I knew it was the last time I would see her I said a prayer at her head and said I love you! I cried the whole drive home but I also felt peace.

At this same time others were have experiences with death. Another close friend Cyndi would call me and tell me the most peaceful of stories. Her grandmother, a very religious Catholic woman, was dying while waiting for the priest to come. The family decided to say The Rosary, bead by bead and then after say goodbyes, thinking she was just asleep. The reality was that she peacefully went during the saying of The Rosary. It helped her make her journey to hear the words she loved from the people she loved most.

My last advice is to never feel guilty that you were not there when someone passed away. Sometimes one passes while you are gone for the simplest of reasons, even to get food or sleep. The journey is how they want it to be and it is not for us to say we should have been there. Some of us want to go when others are not around and others want us around. It happens all like it is supposed to happen so let go of the guilty and negative feelings you have over a loved one's death and try to feel them instead. Remember them as much as you can. Talk about them, buy them presents if you want. Let them be at peace with you to be in balance with this process called death.

Having all these experiences with death from having it hidden from me to being a part of it, I can say that, while being a part of it was hard I must admit, the honor and love I felt somehow makes it okay and worth it. I will never again walk away from the opportunity of helping someone go through the journey. I can also say that after all these experiences, from reading and talking with people like Neale Donald Walsch and Dannion Brinkley, I am not afraid to die. I do not want it to be soon as I feel I still have a lot of work here, but when it happens I will be with making that journey as it will still be my life but without this body. I know it is not the end and that if I live in the present moment now doing my best to help others. I will have done what I was here for and will have no regrets. I hope that all the lives I have touched while being here will remember me with love and feel at peace when they think about me. Someone told me once it's just like getting another body and next time you get to choose what it is you want it to look like. Maybe I will be a Dragonfly next so I can fly around all my loved ones.

Never fear the unknown, only
dream!
--Unknown

People are often unreasonable, illogical, and self-centered; forgive them anyway. If you are kind, people may accuse you of selfish, ulterior motives; be kind anyway. If you are successful, you may win some false friends and some true enemies: succeed anyway. If you are honest and frank, people may cheat you: be honest and frank anyway. What you spend years building, someone could destroy overnight; build anyway. If you find serenity and happiness, others may be jealous; be happy anyway. The good you do today, people will often forget tomorrow; do good anyway. If you give the world the best you have, it may never be enough; give the world the best you've got anyway. You see, in the final analysis, it is between you and God; it was never between you and other people anyway.

'Wisdom to Live by'
--Mother Teresa

The Success OM

Create Success For Yourself – How Can I Be Successful in Today's Economy?

There are seven spiritual laws that if followed will bring on success and abundance, as said by Deepak Chopra. When we follow these laws the energy or universe has to provide it, as it is our birthright and there is enough in this world to take care of us all.

When I started my business it was indeed a struggle to always keep new business following in, new marketing ideas and trusting that it would all just work out. Last December I was having the hardest time keeping my head above water and again trusting that the universe would provide for me. Lots of tests were thrown at me, some of which I passed and some that I failed. In the midst of all of this I came across this book by Mr. Chopra and the idea came to me to create my second CD Mystic Meditations for success and abundance, seven meditations that if listened to would bring on the thinking and patterns without much work. The meditations came easy as it usually does when I am aligned and doing what is right. The first story that came in was a success story of winning the lottery, then one about someone getting a job after years of looking and so on. Again what you want more of you need to give away so in my eyes putting this out into the world for others to become successful helps me to stay successful. After releasing this CD I landed my first TV interview and then ideas flowed about finishing my book, which had been sitting stagnate for so many years.

Now when I hear others talk about why they cannot find work, why their ideas are not working or why their lives are not going anywhere I can see what keeps them stuck. I now can identify what keeps me stuck or why I might have a bad day or week and with this information I am able to turn it around. This is why I am adding in this extra Om in the book, as a bonus for you to start to see what keeps you from being successful and change it. These are my seven ways to create success for yourself in today's economy.

1. *Believe in yourself* – stop all negative talk about who you are and what you can do. You are you the only one like you and you can do anything that you put your mind to. We all have the potential to do what it is we are dreaming of doing. Start to believe this NOW!

2. *Give what you want more of out in the world.* If you want peace then give it. If you want a job then volunteer. I was laid off once and saw an ad about helping a family with their brain-dead child; I called and started to help them every Saturday. Within two weeks I had a new job but continued to stay with them for one year. My mind set was I will do this to help me get a job and it did. If you want love then give it, smile at everyone. Help others when they need it and hug lots of people.

3. *Look at your actions or Karma.* Do you tell the truth? Do you steal? How are you acting in everyday life? Look at these things now. Is this what is stopping you from having success? Remember words are powerful, I hear lots of people say things then when they see the look on my face they say "Oh I was kidding". The laws of attraction do not understand joking around or just making claims for fun. Mean what you say and say what you mean, speaking your truth and being kind will keep your karma clean. Pay your karma forward by giving random acts of kindness every day.

4. *Trust.* This one is a tough one for many and at times for myself as well. Trusting in these energy laws and the fact that the universe is always working in our favor creating what we need. That is working on brining in people, places and situations to help us achieve our goals as long as we are not stepping on our own hose and stopping the flow.

5. *Set an intention or a clear picture.* What is it you are looking for. Seeing a clear picture of what it is you are wanting or asking for is needed in order for the universe to create that for you. If you waver back and forth with different ideas it will confuse the energy and you will get conflicting results.

6. *Detach from the outcome.* We tend to try to force things to happen in the way we want them to happen. Letting go and not having the expectation of how it is supposed to be in our own minds. The universe has all in mind and we may not, so again trust in it to create what is best for all. Go with the flow of it all and don't get stuck in the story.

7. *Find your purpose.* This is one that I think stops a lot of people. Your purpose does not have to be this grand purpose, as most think. It can be to 'just be in the moment' each day, with that being an example for others. Whatever it is, your purpose is only yours and only you can know what that is. Slowing down and meditating will bring you the answers to those kinds of questions.

If you take a look at these and then apply them to your life, there is nothing you cannot accomplish. This world is a magical place and we are magnificent beings. We have the power within ourselves to create all the success and abundance we want. Every successful person whether they understand these laws or not, are using them.

If you think you can, you can.
And if you think you can't,
you're right.
--Mary Kay Ash

The Top 10 Most Important Things list

1 - *Love*
   Unconditional is always true love

2 - *Respect*
   Treating others as if they matter and are loved by you
      See #1 for definition of love

3 - *Appreciation*
   To be grateful for all the blessings you have had in the past, have now and
   will have in the future, no matter how small

4 - *Happiness*
   To feel love for yourself and others
      See #1 for definition of love

5 - *Forgiveness*
   The ability to accept things as they are; it is what it is and to love
      See #1 for definition of love

6 - *Sharing*
   The joy of giving without thought of receiving

7 - *Honesty*
   The quality of always telling the truth, no matter how hard

8 - *Integrity*
   The purity of doing what's right, no matter what

9 - *Compassion*
   The essence of feeling another's pain, while easing their hurt

10 - *Peace*
   The reward for living the 10 Most Important Things

~ ॐ ~

In closing

I thank you for taking time from your life to read my book. I appreciate all the effort it took for you to do the exercises and to enlighten your life. All the work put forth here was positive even if it brought up any negativity for you. Negativity is necessary to see what you are not, to see the other side and so that you can appreciate all that is divine.

Basically, this book teaches you ways to recognize negative or excessive patterns. It teaches you creative and effective ways to release or change them by using your own thoughts and inner power. It explains how you are worthy of giving to yourself and taking care of yourself, with easy exercises to start doing so today. After reading this book continue to do the work by becoming a member on my web-site and doing the exercises that will be on my blog and forum.

When we are in addiction, in powerless thoughts and when life is not working it is just us being disconnected from Spirit, our Spirit, God or whatever you want to call it. Finding your Spirit again will get you back on track and back in the game of life. Meditation is what I feel is missing in our everyday lives, that is how we can reconnect. Within the workbooks I have given you many different ways to do this by focusing on your thoughts and turning your attention inward. This is how I changed my life, my career and how I now can pass it along to help others.

Stop the negative thoughts, actions and patterns and use that energy to create a outstanding expression of yourself. Put it out into the world so that it can help others. Your expression can be art, music, acting, photography, writing, riding horses or whatever it might be. Do it with only your heart in it and the intention of love and healing behind it and you with gain success and abundance from it. Don't waste this life fighting with others around you and the currents of the energy. Flow with it and it will carry you to a place of faith and trust, the ultimate love for yourself.

I would also like to be clear about something else written in this book. I want to elaborate on my Mother a bit. Yes, she has a hard time showing love and letting go, and though I call her the strongest woman I know and this is the truth: you have to be strong to hold love back for so long. But don't get me wrong, I see her showing me love in her own ways. She loves physical things. She's not a materialistic person; she just has collectables and such. She holds onto them and loves them. She is the most awesome gift giver. She buys things then calls me up and says she has no use for something, and it is always something my daughter wanted or something I needed. I do love her very much and do not feel resentment towards anything she has done or not done in my eyes. I can say I feel no anger or resentment towards anyone that has hurt me. How many can say that, I wonder? Do this work and you will be able to say that with confidence. You will be full of love instead of hate, worry, stress and despair. Your life will begin to flow and when you are in the midst of hard bumpy roads ahead you will ride it like a champ and be stronger for it.

When life flows you can enjoy and be grateful for what you have accomplished and are blessed with. Instead of always being in "I want".

If you have fallen off Balance NEVER FEAR. Read this book and do the work. There is no Magic pill! Look at the medications you are taking, talk to your doctor about holistic ways to treat these dis-eases. Then start to Meditate, yes "Meditation instead of Medication", this is what will bring you Balance so you can find your Spirit and love of life. Thank you for the honor of sharing my life's experiences and love. Namaste'.

There is nothing more miraculous than you!
--Debra Lynne Katz

Breathing Meditation
Ojai Breath - A Yogi form of breathing

Use when you need to relax or to bring yourself back into your body and become aware of your breathing. For sitting, standing or lying down.

~ Sit with feet flat on the floor or in crossed legged position. Draw a straight line from sacrum up through the crown of the head. Lift up through the breast bone and let the shoulders fall away from the ears.
~ Stand connecting with the earth through the feet, engaging the thigh muscles, lifting up through the breast bone and letting the shoulders fall away from the ears.
~ Lay down, your arms at your side, feet flat with knees up or extending your legs, whatever feels comfortable for your back.

Inhale in through the nose all the way down to the bottom of the belly. Let the belly rise   and exhale out through parted lips making a 'HA' sound by constricting through the throat while the belly falls. Take in as many breaths as you need to move to relaxation.

Taking Inventory of the Body
Featured in both Melissa Stone's CDs

This is a checking-in with yourself, to use when you are trying to relax the whole body or one part of the body.

Start with Breathing Meditation and become relaxed.

Take inventory in your body. Find where you are holding stress, tension or negativity and send the breath there.

With each inhale surround the stress or tension and using the exhale release it.

Adding in some visualization, see the breath as white light.... your energy or chi, sending it to each stress or tension spot, surrounding the stress or tension and exhale it out feeling and seeing it leave the body.

Start from the crown and slowly move down the body until you feel the body move to total relaxation.

Protection, Strengthen and Healing Meditation
Featured in Melissa's Mystic Meditations for daily life CD

Use daily or when you need to protect your energy, give yourself strength, heal your body, release and re-ground.

Start with the Breathing Meditation and become relaxed. In your mind's eye see yourself floating above and seeing yourself lying or sitting. See white light at the crown of the head. Pull it down past the feet, covering yourself in white light, giving yourself protection. Seeing purple energy at the feet pulling the purple energy up the legs meeting at the base of the spine and out the crown of the head, giving yourself strength. Then see green energy illuminating the heart center, green energy is healing energy. Send the healing energy throughout the body. Float yourself back down but still see yourself covered in a bubble of white light, purple light coming up the body and green energy surrounding the Heart Chakra.

Focusing on the tail bone of the body, the Root Chakra visualize the old root that grounds you. See it coming from the tail bone attaching you to the Earth, just like the root of a plant. In your mind's eye see things that cause you stress, tension or pain and send them to the old root. Taking in a deep cleansing breath using the exhale to release the old root, letting it take away anything that no longer serves you. Take in another cleansing breath. See a new root coming from the tail bone and send it down into the Earth, keeping you centered and grounded.

Sleep Meditation
Featured in Melissa's Mystic Meditations for daily life CD

Use when you are having trouble falling asleep.

Start with Breathing Meditation and become relaxed.
Take inventory in your body until you move to total relaxation.
Start to draw your upside down V
Close the eyes and use your eye lids as your movie screen.
As you inhale draw a line up and as you exhale let that line fall down.
Repeat this process over and over again until you fall asleep.
Remember if you have a hard time clearing your mind, just let the thoughts move in and out like clouds, do not take judgment or action on them.
If you find yourself thinking - as soon as you realize it, move back to the breath.

Letting Go of Stress
Featured in both Melissa Stone's CDs

Use when you are having trouble letting go of stress, a situation or person.

Start with Breathing Meditation and become relaxed.
Take inventory in your body until you move to total relaxation.
Create a symbol of your stress, situation or person.
See it in your mind's eye, and see a cord attached to you like a balloon.
Inhale see it, exhale cut the cord and release it.
See the stress floating away and feel the body relaxing.
If it is something you need to pick back up later, like work.
Then tie the balloon to a tree on the way home from work and pick it back up the next day.

~ It is all a practice, It all counts and it only has to take minutes of your time. ~

Bibliography

Sarah Ban Breathnach, Author
Contact: www.simpleabundance.com
Her book: Simple Abundance: A Daybook of Comfort and Joy

Rhonda Byrne, Author
Contact: www.thesecret.tv; www.whatisthesecret.tv
Her book: The Secret

Edgar Cayce, Author
Contact: **www.edgarcayce.org**
His book: The Sleeping Prophet

Deepak Chopra, MD, Author
Contact: **www.chopra.com**
Some of his books: Grow Younger, Live Longer, The Seven Spiritual
                        Laws of Success, Why is God Laughing and
                        Freedom from Addiction

Bryn C. Collins, M.A., L.P. Author
Her book: Emotional Unavailability: Recognizing It,
                        Understanding It, and Avoiding Its Trap

Debra Lynne Katz, Author
Contact: debrakatz@yahoo.com; Ph: 310-801-0521
www.debrakatz.com, www.urpsychic.com, www.newschoolpsychic.com
Some of her books: You Are Psychic: The Art of Clairvoyant Reading
                        and Healing; Extraordinary Psychic: Proven
                        Techniques to Master Your Natural Psychic
                        Abilities

Dr. Jay Lombard, Author
Contact: 1730 S. Federal Highway, Suite 314; Delray Beach,
                        FL 33483; Tel. 561-654-1300 ; Fax. 561-266-5786;
                        www. drjaylombard.com
Some of his books: Balance Your Brain, Balance Your Life; and The
                        Brain Wellness Plan

Bibliography [continued]

Dr. Judith Orloff, MD, Author
Contact: www.drjudithorloff.com
Some of her books: Positive Energy, Second Sight and Intuitive Healing

Randy Pausch; The Last Lecture
Contact: www.thelastlecture.com
His last work: The Last Lecture in book and video form

Sanaya Roman and Duane Packer, Author
Contact: www.orindaben.com
Some of their books: Opening To Channel: How to Connect With Your
                      Guide; Creating Money: Attracting Abundance

Joyce Schwarz, JCOM
Contact: joyceschwarz@gmail.com; www.ihaveavision.org
Her book: Vision Boards

Neale Donald Walsh, Author
Contact: www.nealedonaldwalsch.com
Some of his books: Conversations with God I, II and III, Home with God
                      and Happier than God

Ruth White, Author
Contact: tigerruth@ruthwhite-gildas.co.uk;
                      www.ruthwhite-gildas.co.uk
Some of her books: Energy Healing for Beginners, Working With Your
                      Soul, Working with Spirit Guides, Chakras - A New
                      Approach to Healing Your Life, Karma and
                      Reincarnation, Working With Guides and Angels,
                      Working With Your Chakras and Your Spiritual
                      Journey

Source School of Tantra Yoga
Contact: 888 6-TANTRA; O Box 368 Kahului, HI
                      96733
                      www.sourcetantra.com

Inner Light Center

Inner Light Ministries is an Omnifaith outreach ministry dedicated to spiritual transformation. We provide "Tools for Living"™ that encourage the practical application of Universal Spiritual Principles to all of life's circumstances. Our aim is healing through the energy of love and the revealing of our own Inner Light. As an Omnifaith ministry, we embody Spiritual Oneness, appreciate individualized expressions, and honor all paths that lead to Truth.

Located:	5630 Soquel Drive; Soquel, California
Contact:	Phone: 831-465-9090; Fax: 831-465-0301
	Outside 831 Area Code: 800-933-0920
	Email: ilm@innerlightministries.com;
	www.innerlightministries.com

Cypress Health Institute
Massage school

Located:	21511 East Cliff Dr Santa Cruz CA 95062
Contact:	831-476-2115; www.cypresshealthinstitute.com

Pacific Healing Arts (Santa Cruz Chi Center)
Healing Clinic

Contact:	831-465-9088; www.leeholden.com

The Camp Recovery

Located:	3192 Glen Canyon Rd; Scotts Valley CA 66569
Contact:	831-438-1868; www.camprecovery.com

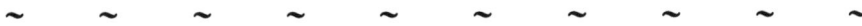

~   ~   ~   ~   ~   ~   ~   ~   ~   ~

Musicals

Metaphysical Musicals
Onebody

Created by:	Coventry, James
Directed by:	Neale Donald Walsch
	www.onebodytheatrecompany.com

~ ॐ ~

About the author

Melissa A. Stone is a CMT and Certified Fitness Professional.

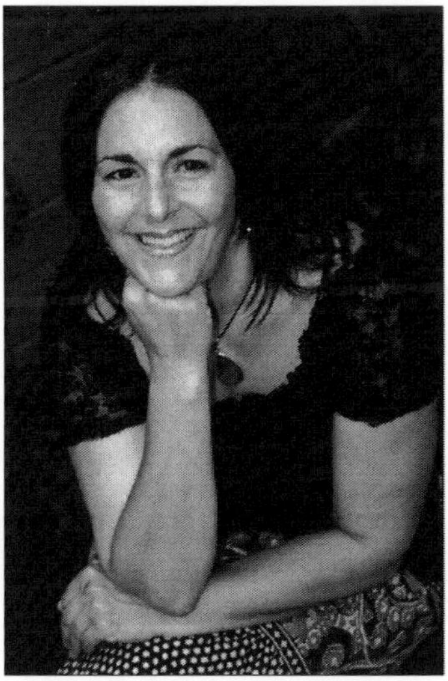

Her clients say she has a healer's touch and a psychic's intuition. She says it is the intention – her intention is that of helping in the healing of others. Sending out this intention bringing us all to the goal of oneness and balance - World PEACE!

Melissa understands how to stand aside and let Spirit work through her, channeling her guided meditations and writings from the other side, in order to help those with stress, sleep, weight, addiction and depression issues.

Photo by: Clarissa Guggenheim
Guggenheim@gmail.com

As the proprietor of Balance Studio Spa, a successful full service holistic fitness and wellness spa in the Santa Cruz Mountains of California - she has produced two DVDs and two CDs and co - hosted a radio talk show. Melissa is frequently quoted and has several articles published on the subject of holistic health. Her focus and intention is that of helping others find balance in their lives, using tools including fitness, body/energy-work, meditation and nutrition.
She knows what it feels like to be overweight, depressed and lacking in self esteem. After suffering for years she took matters into her own hands. Finding a yoga and Pilates practice was just the beginning of a life long journey towards wellness. A graduate from Cypress Health Institute - Santa Cruz, CA along with completing many other classes in massage, polarity and fitness. Gaining the knowledge of a whole holistic practice that includes exercise, body/energy-work, and meditation. Re-shaping her own body and her life using these tools, she decided to give back and pass on this knowledge to help others. In 2003 she left her twenty year long career working in the corporate

setting to open Balance Studio Spa, in the mountains of Santa Cruz and work at her life's path.

Melissa found the key to changing her life, was to change the way the energy flowed through her body. Gathering the energy and clearing her own energy blocks allowing the healing energy to flow openly though her, changing her path. These energy centers (found in the Chakra System or central nervous system) are her focus when working with clients. Helping them to understand what the Chakras are and how to recognize when they are out of balance is the key to putting them back in balance. She has designed exercise classes, workshops, guided meditations and her own line of Home Practice Products that all target the Chakra System to bring the body, mind and spirit back in balance. Melissa also writes for Belly Dance Magazine www.bellydancemag.com

Home Practice Products from Melissa Stone:
Mystic Meditations DVD
Mystic Meditations CD for daily life
Mystic Meditations CD for success and abundance
Groovy Goddess Workout – Yoga and Pilates

And her holistic fitness and wellness spa
Balance Studio Spa
www.balancestudiospa.com

~ॐ~

Cover art work

When I saw what I wanted the cover to look like in my mind's eye I knew that there was only one person that could draw what I saw. I am honored that Gary Winnick took the time to make the cover to my book.

Gary Winnick has worked as an artist, designer and art director. He began his professional career as an assistant to noted comic book illustrator Neal Adams. Later Gary worked for nine years as an artist, animator and art director at Lucasfilm and Lucasarts, where he co-designed the noted graphic adventure 'Maniac Mansion'. At Lucas he was also creator and supervising producer of 'Defenders of Dynatron City' which aired as an animated special on the Fox kids network.

Photo by: Clarissa Guggenheim
Guggenheim@gmail.com

Currently, Gary serves as a creative director as at his own company Lightsource Studios, a bay area contract art studio whose clients have included Yahoo!, Electronic Arts and Disney.

Gary's website: www.Lightsourcestudios.com; gary@lightsourcestudios.com

~   ~   ~   ~   ~   ~   ~   ~   ~

Editing and Graphic Arts

Debi Burdman-Deutsch has been editing and proofreading for over thirty years and has been working with graphic arts for over ten years, and is thrilled to participate in the creation of Melissa's excellent book.
Contact: singerdancer3@yahoo.com

Photo by: Photography by BOB
BobSBd@comcast.net

~ ॐ ~

Published by:

Dragonfly Publishing Company
www.dragonflypublishingcompany.com
© October 11, 2008 -- all rights reserved
'Weekly Om' is a trademark of Balance Studio Spa

2081210

Made in the USA